Driving Demand

The CODE for SALES

Elizabeth Allen

ISBN-10: 1502999900

ISBN-13: 978-1502999900

Table of Contents

Foreword: Why I Love This Book 5

Why Change? 7

Get Every Employee Engaged 9

Chapter One: Why Change? 13

What Change Looks Like 25

Chapter Two: What Is CODE? 27

How to Implement Change 39

Chapter Three: the Psychology of CODE 41

Chapter Four: First Steps to Implementation 57

Chapter Five: Develop the Marketing Action Plan (MAP) 63

Chapter Six: Convert to Yellow-Blue-Red (YBR) 73

Chapter Seven: Achieve Cultural Change 89

Chapter Eight: Work the YBR Pipeline 103

Chapter Nine: Progress Meetings and Driving Accountability 123

Chapter Ten: CODE and Technology 137

Afterword 149

Tips & Tools 153

Implementation Tips 155

Frequently Asked Questions 163

A Sample YBR Progress Meeting Agenda 171

Dear Employees, Here's What's in It for You 173

Cheat Sheet: CODE Snapshot for Personal Use ... 181

Foreword: Why I Love This Book

By Michael E. Gerber

Yes, I do love this book. In fact, I wish I had written it. I believe you're going to love it too, for exactly the same reasons that I do.

And that's because in this book, Elizabeth Allen has struck the impossible chord... a resonant response to a universal problem in all companies... how to standardize the unstandardizable. She has shown how to turn-key the seemingly too-sophisticated process through which any company can, with great predictability, identify its most important prospects, convert them into champions, and deliver to them with certainty and conviction, no matter who in the company is accountable for the process. Provided, of course, that the accountable ones have learned, internalized, integrated and implemented in their practice what Elizabeth calls so resolutely, and, I might say, religiously, "The CODE."

Yes, Elizabeth Allen's "CODE" is a religion of sorts for those who have internalized it.

A religion, because The CODE has this uncanny way of signifying the truth.

Once you read The CODE, and apply it to your company, you will immediately see why your client acquisition capability up to this point in time—the time you are confronted with The CODE—leaves so much to be desired.

And that's because without The CODE, there is no certainty in what you do.

Without The CODE, there is no replicable method for producing consistent, significantly above average results in your company.

Without The CODE, there is no objective measure for quantifying client acquisition activities across your sales organization, let alone in accounting, operations, or any other function within your organization which struggles with the question: what can we depend upon today, tomorrow, or next month?

The CODE answers that question, and many more just like it, with the clarity of a ringing bell.

So, thank you, Elizabeth Allen, for introducing me to The CODE— and for introducing The CODE to your readers.

I know it will become exactly that kind of book that stays with us for years and years. A brilliant classic. A stunning epiphany. A profoundly original contribution and work.

—Michael E. Gerber
Author of *Awakening the Entrepreneur Within* and *The E-Myth books*
Carlsbad, California

Why Change?

Get Every Employee Engaged

Now, every person must drive demand.

Do you walk down the halls of your company and fantasize about getting people to sell better because your own personal job security or the future of the company depends on it?

In the past, companies could get away with the bologna statement that "We're all in sales!"—*wink wink, nod nod*—without holding themselves accountable. *Guess what, folks?*

Those days are over.

If you've been conscious and breathing during the past ten years, you know the world has become hyperconnected and hypercompetitive. It's an entirely new game.

To win that game, every company must now drive demand by deliberately deploying every person to sell with the confidence of an entrepreneur. Why? Because whether we like it or not—or are ready or not—each one of us is now an economy of one. We must justify our organizational cost by driving demand for what we can uniquely supply. It's the final evolution of the "flat organization." If we're not selling professionally for the company we work for, we still have to learn these personal entrepreneurial selling skills for ourselves. Why? Two reasons:

1. By 2019, the U.S. Department of Labor projects that 40% of the workforce will be contract-based employees or free agents.[1] Experts from Fast Company suggest it's more like 70%.

2. Up to 47% of all jobs will be automated out of existence in the next two decades or so.[2]

No matter how secure your job seems today, you must consider how to develop alternative income streams and security for your family. These are uncertain economic times. Things are rapidly changing.

How many of us have a kid living in the basement, looking for a job or internship, 80% of which are not posted? How many of us have kids graduating from college and now facing a 53% unemployment or underemployment rate?[3]

Now, the question, "What's in it for me to learn to think, act and sell like an entrepreneur?" is painfully obvious. Entrepreneurs are opportunity creators, and the new game favors people who are skilled at leveraging relationships to create their own opportunities. Native to this environment, the millennial generation is one of the most entrepreneurial on record.[4]

It's time to start an honest and open dialogue with your employees about adopting an entrepreneurial mindset in order to drive demand for your company products. You need sustainable and dynamic cultural change. So do they.

---

[1] Greenwald, Richard. "To Boost the Economy, Help the Self-Employed." *Bloomberg Businessweek.* 7 June 2001. Web. 23 Oct. 2014.
[2] Frey, Carl, and Michael Osborne. "The Future of Employment: How Susceptible Are Jobs to Computerisation?" University of Oxford. 17 Sept. 2013. Web. 12 Oct. 2014.
[3] Weissmann, Jordan. "53% of Recent College Grads Are Jobless or Underemployed—How?" *The Atlantic.* 23 Apr. 2012. Web. 12 Oct. 2014.
[4] "Gen Y on the Job." *Payscale.* Web. 12 Oct. 2014.

What about the people who can't sell? Well, at a bare minimum, they need to learn to nurture relationships, or as sales people call it, "farm." One of the CEOs I worked for put it this way: "If you can't communicate with people or care for relationships, you probably don't have a job here."

Relationship management skills are a new minimum requirement for employment. They represent a true definition of the term "social selling."

The good news? **People want to learn these skills.** If properly positioned, people are motivated. They have a lot to gain by adapting. They realize they need to leverage relationships. They need to use who they know to connect to who they want to know, in order to identify and ask for new income opportunities, internships or jobs.

This book squarely addresses the question of change: why we need it, what it looks like and how to engage in it right now. There is no margin of error. While you will find thousands of books written about sales, none addresses what *Driving Demand* does: how to align the *entire* organization for the purpose of selling, no matter what type of work you do or your workflow.

Entrepreneurs make the most compelling model for successful sales behaviors. They start with who they know, what they know and where they stand *today*.[5] They embody what it takes to be an economy of one. Give your organization—and yourself—permission to be one, too.

This book will equip you to lead your entire company, small or large, to sell successfully as a team, no matter your existing workflow processes, data structures or corporate culture.

It's a "how-to" book your company can go to war with—and win.

---

[5] Taylor, Bill. "MBAs vs. Entrepreneurs: Who Has the Right Stuff for Tough Times?" *Harvard Business Review.* 4 May 2009. Web. 23 Oct. 2014.

Ready? Put on your seatbelt.

Chapter One: Why Change?

Surely you've heard the mantra: "We're all in sales!"

Indeed we are, but most companies have found no real way to drive accountability to that goal. The result? Rainmakers are exhausted, entrepreneurial leaders lack an exit strategy and a few die-hard warriors maintain the pipeline (and are expected to continually feed the beast). For the last decade, I've worked with and studied companies desperately struggling with these issues. Guess what? They are just like yours.

Enter *#social media.* In the blink of a few .coms, the game changed. *Again.*

This tired mantra of "We are all in sales!" holds true now more than ever, because everyone we know *professionally* is connected to us *personally* online. The hard little red line that separates our personal and professional lives is completely blurred, because we are highly visible and digitally tracked every time we log on. Thanks to companies like LinkedIn, our employees are now personally connected to our strategic partners, vendors, prospects and core customers in a maze of touch points, which are meticulously mined by social platforms that harness the firepower of big data.

Technology has rendered employees armed and dangerous. Make no mistake; these engines require *context* to mine your *content.* They are focused on the quality of your relational ties over the quantity of your "likes." The aim is to identify *exactly* what drives loyalty and trust. These engines are intent on extracting every insight into *why* people prefer to do business with you-the-company and specifically, with you-the-person. Companies need a plan to more strategically manage and protect their relational networks. Without proactive efforts to protect their relational IP, technology snipers are happy to walk away with this extraordinary bounty of company data.

Executives have often steered clear of digital danger by keeping it at a personal distance. The higher in the organization you go, the more they opt out of visibility. But increasingly, this response isn't viable in a world that uses searches to verify our identity. That's because Invisible = Irrelevant.

Our corporate ability to compete in the war for talent depends on the online transparency of our companies and leaders. A few top tech companies dictate our relevance, both personally and professionally. They remind us *at every turn* that the most junior-level hire is now a brand ambassador, a truly human expression of what the company *hopes* its customers and allies value most. Increasingly but unwittingly, employees are the faces and voices of the companies they work for—online and off.

I'm not talking here about the idea of a comprehensive social media policy. I'm also not talking about "social selling" as the buzz defines it today (lead generation plus content creation and curation).

Instead, I'm talking about a strategy to manage and mine social currency across the organizational ranks. Who do your people know? Who can they get to know? Everyone needs a clear understanding of their personal and relational responsibilities in caring for core customers and in hunting for new ones.

It's time to do "the impossible." It's time for everyone to focus on *managing relationships differently* so that the tasks associated with generating referrals (farming) and identifying new business (hunting) are easy to manage and produce new opportunity across the organization. It's time to drive demand for what it is you can uniquely supply by using every person with relational assets in your organization. Not just the exhausted sales team.

Here's the key question: are you ready for this as a company? Are your employees? What's your plan?

If you feel like a deer in the headlights, you've found the right book.

Sales & Relationships: The "S" Word and the "R" Word

Sales. There, I said it.

Have you ever noticed that when you say "sales," people tend to immediately fall into one of two camps? It's the "Love it!" or "Hate it!" effect, with little in between. Surely, you know what I'm talking about. By simply uttering the word, people immediately think of a schmooze fest with a greasy side of insincerity. This reaction makes me hate using the word, but out of respect for the discipline, let's call a spade a spade.

The sales process I present is entrepreneurial at heart. It delivers a step-by-step approach anyone can understand. While it focuses on sales as a measurable outcome, the bottom line is that it will enhance relational management skills across the organization.

I call this simple process CODE. That stands for Communicate, Organize, Document, Evaluate. I designed it to help employees identify, manage and care for priority relationships critical to the company's success. What I discovered is that while CODE works for companies, it also delivers value for individuals struggling to nurture relationships, too. This book is about what CODE does for companies. I wrote another one—*Economy of One*—to teach individuals how to use CODE to grow long-term relationships and to generate opportunities for themselves and their families. In both cases, relationships are everything.

One CEO confessed to me, "You know what makes me lose sleep? Anxiety over how, at any given moment, some employee, somewhere, might mismanage a relationship with one of our key clients. We need a clear way to answer the question, 'When was the last time we were in front of each of our core customers in a meaningful way?' That's what keeps me up at night." If you're in management, you know what he's talking about.

How do you get past the tired line, "The customer comes first," and entice them to go above and beyond to create and cultivate new and existing customer relationships? How do you turn your junior hire into a rainmaker? How do you light a fire under *every single employee* to build and reinforce relational connections—a fire that the C-suite already feels and knows to be paramount to success?

You do it the same way you get anyone to learn something new: show them *what's in it for them* when they master the new skill set.

Unlike most sales strategies aimed solely at enriching the company, CODE has a second purpose: to teach employees to use the same tools for cultivating relationships in their own networks. Something is directly in it for them. CODE doesn't come with incentives; CODE *is* an incentive.

Employees readily adopt CODE to help their companies once they see the company is adopting CODE to help them. Usually about midway through training, a mental light bulb goes off as the employees realize, "I can use this to generate my own opportunities. I can use this to create income for my family or help my kids find jobs or internships. This isn't just how my company can thrive in the new economy—this is how *I* can do well, too." Once that realization sinks in, employees possess a personal reason to build new client relationships that goes far beyond "My boss told me to do this."

If considerable anxiety has pulsed through your company during the past few years of economic uncertainty, instituting a defined structure can be very reassuring. As one employee put it at a company I consulted for,

"We were pleased that our company was putting into place a lead generation program as families were facing layoffs without work. We absolutely knew this, but no one wanted to talk about it. It gave us comfort to know management had a plan and was asking us to step up and help, even though we didn't really 'see' ourselves in sales."

CODE is simple to understand because I've found *less* is so much more. I can teach it in a 90-second video, an hour-long e-learning platform, or an 8-hour intensive presentation. It just depends on how deep participants want to go in understanding the details. The key concepts are so "Keep It Simple, Stupid!" that anybody (including my fifth grade kid) can understand them, put them into practice and start producing results.

When you begin making the switch to CODE, both you and your employees will stand in the same place as entrepreneurs do when they are first starting out. Take a deep breath! Know that entrepreneurs start where you are today: with what and who they know. We'll do the same thing.

What people don't often say about entrepreneurs is that they give themselves permission to move forward, no matter how they feel in the moment and no matter how uncertain the road. *They know it will be messy.* They know it may be uncomfortable at times, but they proceed anyway.

Building relationships is the same. You have to start somewhere. It's time for organizations to be as intentional with relationships as they are with every other business process. Your company and its employees need a way to consolidate a comprehensive relational inventory. With an inventory, you'll be able to start leveraging the strength of unrecognized relational ties, like that brother of an employee's college roommate who happens to be a decision-maker at your dream client. With a dynamic, relational map, when someone you know meets someone you want to know, *you'll know!*

CODE measures relational return on investment across the entire organization. You'll know the relational ROI of every employee, and, the potential relational ROI of every new hire if they opt-in to CODE.

Imagine being able to look at two equally qualified engineers and objectively quantify the potential value their relationships could add to your company. Beyond looking at skills and experience, you'll hire, train and retain your workforce with the clarity of knowing exactly how each individual increases your company's collective social currency and sales.

Too often, I've witnessed corporate dry heaves set in when a company vice president realizes that long-term secretary Doris, who sits down the hall, has a beloved brother-in-law, Ben, at the company they just sent a multi-million dollar proposal. Much to their dismay and *far too late to do squat about it*, they learn that Ben also happens to be the decision maker.

I've seen this actually happen. The company uncovered the key Relationship—the "R" word—too late in the game. Relationship was the critical link that would have made the difference in the sale. But no one thought to ask the lowly secretary about who she knows. Companies must engage a more effective solution to avoid such Titanic acts of stupidity.

Now is the time to do it. We need to get over hang-ups about the "S" word and the "R" word. If you are serious about growing your company's sales, then map and leverage every connectional tie in the whole company (not just the ones on your sales team), build relationships with people you know and engage those you want to know. This is how entrepreneurs find their first clients and break new ground in business development. It's also the most efficient way that individuals drum up jobs and opportunities for themselves.

This leads to my next question: how do you *really* feel about aligning everyone in the organization to truly engage with sales? Uneasy? Uncertain? I'm asking you directly because your future and that of your company depend entirely on your response. How willing are you to be held accountable to the maxim, "We are *all* in sales"?

As you ponder my question, I can hear the roaring chorus of issues and excuses lifting their hoary little heads in your mind...

- When I mention the "S" word, people freak out. Few like to think of themselves in sales, much less consider it a snappy new part of their job. Are you kidding me?

- What do you think we already do all day? We are as lean as it gets. Add one more thing to the plate and someone might go postal.

- Do you realize how hard we've already struggled with this? Consider the act of Congress it took to implement CRM and get our employees to adopt it. It was like trying to herd cats at nap time. We are already exhausted and we haven't even started.

- What's in it to change? Really, lady. *Why, why, why go down this path?*

I'll tell you why. Like no other time in history, employees need to think like entrepreneurs and know how to sell because they (and their children) face a most uncertain future. The economy is shifting, structurally, and so is the nature of employment. The long-term, solid, lifelong job is becoming a myth, replaced by a swarm of free agents who lean on their relational networks to find opportunities for themselves and their families. Soon, one out of every two workers will shuffle from contract to contract. They'll constantly leverage relationships that are their lifeline to new opportunities, since about 80% of jobs are *never* posted.

In an article in *The Wall Street Journal*, entitled "The Age of Going Solo," Dr. Richard Greenwald wrote about this massive shift and said,

> *"The implications for the American workplace are profound. Imagine one in four workers, of all collars, working on a contingent basis. Whole career paths and professions have shifted from stable full-time jobs with definable ca-*

reer ladders and benefits to almost completely contingent work forces that shift from project to project."[6]

Oxford University academics recently concluded that up to 47% of *all jobs* will be automated sometime in the next two decades.[7] When you open up a meeting on this subject, if you present just these two facts—the automated job percentage and contingency worker statistic—alongside a viable solution, you'll have no trouble catching people's attention.

These facts about the structural move to a free agent economy suggest that we must collectively adapt our skills and move to higher ground. The people and companies who will make that climb are those who master the entrepreneurial art of creating new opportunities for themselves through relational networks.

That's why *every* employee needs to sell like an entrepreneur. Why will employees adopt this? Armed with the right motive (providing for the family in a free agent economy) and a solution, employees will listen and understand your rationale for asking them to change. Employees adopt CODE because they recognize the benefits that accompany learning to sell their skills like an entrepreneur in a contract-based, free agent economy:

- Job security and transferrable skills. In global demand, the Sales Representative is the #3 most wanted skill set.[8] *It's really hard to be laid off when you're a rainmaker.*

- Relational marketing skills are the catalyst for growing a vibrant network of allies who can find an unadvertised internship opportunity—or job—for that recent college graduate living in your basement.

---

[6] Greenwald, Richard. "How to Succeed in the Age of Going Solo." *The Wall Street Journal.* 8 Feb. 2010. Web. 12 Oct. 2014.

[7] Frey, Carl, and Michael Osborne. "The Future of Employment: How Susceptible Are Jobs to Computerisation?" University of Oxford. 17 Sept. 2013. Web. 12 Oct. 2014.

[8] "2014 Talent Shortage Survey Results." Manpower Group. Web. 19 Oct. 2014.

- Self-defense for you and those you care about. If you take a quick employee survey and ask how many have been part of a family business, have moonlighted on the side, have a spouse or significant other in transition or have considered starting a small business, you will typically hit a 90%+ response rate. All of these people know from painful experience that nothing matters operationally if you don't have predictable sales. If you approach them properly, you will motivate people to learn this process because it speaks to their past or their present. They will understand it's worth learning, even if it amounts to nothing more than a self-defense mechanism to pass on to people in their networks who may be desperately in need of help.

- Options. A recent LinkedIn survey suggests 80% of all employees are passively looking at opportunities.[9] This is a dirty little secret everyone knows, but no one wants to discuss. Yet, when people learn to think and act with the confidence of an entrepreneur, no one feels trapped. Yes, obviously people know they need employment options. It is in their best interest to start practicing entrepreneurial thinking and selling behaviors on the company dime now, before they are faced with the possibility of having to learn on their own, no matter what their motivations.

Four generations now occupy the workplace, complicating the relational puzzle even more. If you combine these facts with Reid Hoffman's observation that millennials are taking a "tour of duty approach to employment,"[10] lasting an average of two years at each stop, you've run into a huge neon sign that reads:

[9] Petrone, Paul. "Survey Reveals How to Attract Passive Candidates." *ERE.net.* 1 Sept. 2014. Web. 12 Oct. 2014.
[10] Hoffman, Reid, Ben Casnocha, and Chris Yeh. "Tours of Duty: The New Employer-Employee Compact." *Harvard Business Review.* June 2013. Web. 12 Oct. 2014.

Companies need a serious, integrated relational strategy.

Organizations need to offer practical solutions for millennials who are trying to build customer trust and adapt to corporate culture norms. We must measure behaviors, build attitudes and enhance skills that build trust and loyalty with customers. At a minimum, everyone needs to know how to effectively "farm" or generate referrals, as well as to nurture good will.

Millennials are one of the most entrepreneurial generations ever to walk this planet. It's high time that employers recognize this fact and play to its strength by teaching them the entrepreneurial selling skills they readily desire and *value.*

For employers, this game is about pipeline predictability, being proactive instead of reactive and developing an exit strategy. For employees, it's about job security, transferrable skills and fresh options. It's time to model ourselves after entrepreneurs and get to higher ground, because the storm has already started.

The good news? You've got in your hands a highly tested method that integrates well with what you are already doing. It simplifies and clarifies your strategies so that every employee can use their relationships to sell effectively. That's what CODE does.

Most people don't read business, leadership or sales books cover to cover. Bearing that in mind, I organized this book according to the way most busy people read these days. I've broken it down so that no matter where you play on the organizational chart, something actionable awaits you on these pages.

For Organizational Leaders

If you want a bird's eye overview of the issues, you've just read the most important section. Now you know *why* your company needs to change. The next section, "What Is CODE?" will give you the big picture of what you're about to implement.

For Managers Who Are Leading the Charge across the Organization

If you are the implementing CODE in the trenches, the "How to Engage" and "Tips and Tools" areas are designed to make the process seamless. While I aimed the book at your experience, you can point stakeholders to these sections if you are looking to generate more cultural buy-in. You will also find a letter at the back I wrote directly to employees so they will know what's in it for them.

Changing the Perspective & Culture: Yes, It Can Be Like Peeling an Onion

CODE is a cultural change process as much as a business process. The more employees engage, the more CODE changes their mindset and perspective about the nature of work, the purpose of relationships and the value of their company. CODE won't just change what they do; it will change how they think and how they value themselves and their professional relationships. CODE is simple and easy to grasp, yet has many layers, like an onion.

Most people who learn to practice CODE pass through several "light bulb" moments as they suddenly grasp an idea from a new angle. Often this happens when they are putting the idea into practice. For this reason, I touch on key concepts, tools and ideas repeatedly in each section. That way, you will achieve more than learning the theory behind a concept: you will equip yourself to identify, apply and practice the principles behind it.

What Change Looks Like

Chapter Two: What Is CODE?

A litany of shiny new selling ideas, concepts and technologies blows through the business world today. The current buzz it's made includes social selling, the notion that "we are all in marketing" and enabling brand ambassadorship. The list goes on and on. If you are in marketing, sales or leadership, these concepts may sound like white noise because it's so loud. Yet, very few of the repetitive themes adequately anchor the trends to a cohesive vision of where we are collectively headed.

Let me re-frame the challenge for you. These catalysts are fueling the seamless integration of marketing, sales and IT. One of the most direct yet compelling summaries I've seen that addresses all of the emerging trends and technologies is this:

Sales now aren't business-to-business (B2B) or business-to-consumer (B2C). Sales are human-to-human or H2H.[11]

What does this change really look like in the marketplace? It's best captured by the idea that everyone is now part of the sales process, because we are all hyperconnected to one another.

Strategically, *who we know* is connected to *who we want to know*. Selling effectively means systematically managing and mining

---

[11] Kramer, Bryan. "There Is No More B2B or B2C: There Is Only Human to Human (H2H)." *Social Media Today.* 28 Jan. 2014. Web. 23 Oct. 2014.

our relationships. Every employee must use their relationships to sell themselves and your products. This is H2H sales. Your team's relational reach holds the keys to your company's growth potential.

While social selling speaks to the idea of using social media to generate leads, let's state the obvious: those who are generating opportunities could also qualify and pitch those opportunities, or at a minimum, know how to ask their organization for help.

Does the average individual have all the skills required to generate, qualify, pitch and close an opportunity? *Usually not.* Somewhere between the social media post and your balance sheet, it completely falls apart.

If we need every employee to build relationships that lead to sales, but only some employees have any training or interest in doing it, how do we get the entire company on board?

1. Demonstrate there is something in it for them: namely, marketable survival skills for a free agent economy. (Communicate)

2. Assign people specific sales roles that match both their capabilities and their interests. (Organize)

3. Coordinate the team with clear and simple progress tools. (Document)

4. Measure your efforts in an accountable way. (Evaluate)

This is C–O–D–E. Communicate, Organize, Document and Evaluate.

To run any business process well, you have to do these things. The question is, how do you do them consistently with your sales pipeline? How do you get *every* employee to opt in and open his or her relational connections to the team's sales process? How do you produce measurable *and predictable* results to maintain a constant, steady pipeline, instead of a feast-or-famine cycle of sporadic sales? Let's break down the sales cycle in terms of the phases of opportunities, employee roles, team organizing tools and your ultimate goal. Your sales production machine isn't some obscure mystery. You and your people create and maintain it by what you do, every day, in your customer relationships.

CODE Components: Four Phases, Three Roles, Two Tools and One Goal (4-3-2-1)

The good news? Your company is already following CODE, as any company engaged in B2B sales follows these four phases. CODE works in **Four Phases**: lead generation, qualifying opportunities, pitching opportunities and post-sale follow-up.

CODE assigns **Three Roles** (Prospector, Technical Expert, and Closer) to handle opportunities at each phase. CODE organizes your team's efforts using **Two Tools**: a MAP of the company's current and potential relationships; and a Yellow-Blue-Red (YBR) pipeline of where each opportunity stands in the sales process at any given moment. The point? **One Goal**: to keep your pipeline filled and moving predictably.

Four Phases

The Four Phases help your team communicate more effectively about how to manage opportunities. One of the biggest issues in sales is that a "great lead" to one person might be an opportunity no one has qualified yet to someone else. This range of vocabulary only loosely relates to your bottom-line and it's a constant source of frustration for sales managers. CODE clarifies the language so everyone on your team is on the same page about exactly what's happening next with any opportunity at any time.

Three Roles

To manage your opportunity pipeline effectively, assign every employee a clear role that comes with measureable tasks and responsibilities. That way, they know how you expect them to individually support the pipeline.

When you company starts the process of implementing CODE, you will take a quick skills inventory of your people, relating their skills to the three sales roles CODE identifies: Prospector, Technical Expert and Closer. Assign each employee one of those roles. No matter what their job title, every employee can support farming and/or hunting for new opportunities as identified by management.

Who does what when everyone sells?

1) Prospect for new business

Review participating departments or people in the program and identify a list of Prospectors. Who on your team is in the know or in a position to ask about new work? A referral? To be a Prospector? To effectively farm or hunt?

Assign those involved in sales or business development roles as Prospectors. Now consider the secondary key question: are they farming core relationships, hunting for new opportunities or both?

Expand your search for Prospectors across the organization. Will everyone be a Prospector? Not necessarily. Who could be? Who is in a position to nurture key relationships, ask simple questions and secure relational loyalty?

Consider every person in the company as a possibility, for two reasons: first, because you never know who your employees might be connected to. Second, because it's realistic to think that everyone can make a few calls each week to core customers to say hello and thank them for their business. Identify the natural prospectors among your employees.

2) Use technical expertise to explain your solutions

After identifying prospectors, consider who best fits the role of a Technical Expert. In professional fields, anyone who does the actual work is considered a technical expert. Who are the ones that scope projects and estimate service for work performed?

These are your Technical Experts. They are skilled at qualifying an opportunity to determine if it's a good fit for your company. Identify your Technical Experts and invite them to participate in the program.

3) Negotiate final contracts and closing sales

Finally, ask the question: who on our team or in our department is a Closer? A Closer has the authority and ability to negotiate and close deals effectively. Identify who your Closers are and then assign them this role in the sales process.

Three Roles, One Team of Early Adapters

Some people may be pure Prospectors. They lack any type of specific technical skill or closing talent. Others may be pure Technical Experts without prospecting skills or the ability to close. (These are usually the people who say they "hate" sales… even though they love sharing their expertise, which is always critical to landing a sale!) You'll find other employees may fit best as Closers or may even embody the skills of all three roles.

While people may eventually migrate into other roles, start with their capabilities as they exist *today*. It's much simpler to assign people to roles that match their capabilities than to try to change their natural affinities. Consider who in the organization can play the roles of Prospector, Technical Expert and Closer. Ask them to consider supporting this effort.

You need the buy-in of early adapters to secure long-term change. Who is most motivated to change? Consider beginning your implementation efforts with one team of early adapters and then expanding to include the rest of your organization. Early adapters will help you work the kinks out at the beginning. They will help you champion the CODE process to their peers—the employees you want to use CODE.

Two Tools for Your Team

Once you have assigned roles and assembled a team of early adapters, use our eLearning materials or otherwise introduce the CODE process to the team by giving them this section of the book to read. They are about to coordinate their sales efforts with two basic tools: the MAP and the YBR.

Marketing Action Plan (MAP)

The MAP is a detailed list of who we know and who we want to know. Each week, you'll generate several names from the MAP and assign them to team members through a White List. (We call it a White list because each name represents a "blank slate" of opportunity.) Then, the Prospectors will have a week to farm and hunt these blank slates accordingly. You probably have some form of a MAP in your CRM or company database already.

Our MAP features a consolidated relational inventory and applies a numerical relational ranking to each individual contact. The relational rankings are very simple:

1 = We don't know this contact. (Admit it. There are people in the database we really don't even know.)

2 = We know them, but they've given us no business.

3 = They've shortlisted us. There's competition, but we still have opportunity.

4 = They single source us. They are loyal to us.

5 = They send us referrals.

The breakthrough with assigning relational rankings is that it allows companies to track relational progress over time. It gives you a tangible way to examine relational return on investment. You can go beyond measures of "customer satisfaction" and measure the relational loyalty of customers over time. These rankings address critical questions such as, "Is their relationship with your company really growing?" Or, "How effective have your team's efforts been at strengthening those relationships over time?"

Yellow-Blue-Red (YBR)

The second tool used in conjunction with the MAP is the YBR, or Yellow-Blue-Red Pipeline. It's a simple list of all your current sales opportunities. We decided to overlay it with color because research suggests color may improve adult learning and retention by as much as 80-90%.

Pre-pipeline:

Whites = The short list of potential relationships lifted from your MAP. It's everyone you already know *and* everyone you want to know. Prospectors reference white lists to farm and hunt opportunities to add to the pipeline.

In the pipeline:

Yellows = *Confirmed* opportunities that Prospectors uncover by talking to names on the white list. The potential customer says they are looking for a solution in the near future—a solution you know you might be able to provide. But because they lack a budget, timeline or urgency, they are not ready to move on it yet.

Blues = *Definite* opportunities that exist right now. You've confirmed that the potential customer has both a timeline and budget to purchase a solution to fit their needs. They are willing to meet to discuss details. Now, qualify the opportunity. You need a Technical Expert to meet with the prospect to determine if what they are looking for matches the solution you can provide (or if their definition of value matches your definition of price).

Reds = *Fully qualified* opportunities. You have asked the right questions and determined that you can provide them with what they need. They've asked for a proposal, bid, list of qualifications or quotation. It's time to identify a Closer to seal the deal.

Post-pipeline:

Greens = *Closed* opportunities, whether won or lost. Follow-up with greens to find out how the solution that they eventually purchased (yours or another's) is working for them. Keep the relationships growing, regardless of their decision to purchase.

Your current opportunities to make a sale—the Yellows, the Blues and the Reds—make up your sales pipeline, or what we just call the YBR.

Different Stages of the Sale Require Different Skills

Have you ever considered the skills required to move a prospect through the pipeline? Most companies have never broken it down to this level. The advantage of using the YBR is that simple definitions indicate to everyone the behaviors and "next steps" required to move an opportunity forward. Colors provide you with universal definitions so that, with a quick glance, everyone understands exactly where things stand in the pipeline and what's needed to move the opportunity forward most effectively.

With the keep-it-simple clarity of the YBR, teams can coordinate so that the team member with the right skill set attends to the opportunity at the appropriate stage of the sales process. The YBR also clarifies what's *really* a "hot lead" and what isn't. You can view your team's priorities as you juggle opportunities to maintain a steady and predictable flow of revenue and workload.

A healthy sales team has one goal: to keep the pipeline full and moving forward predictably, measurably and effectively. Your bottom line depends on it.

Learn CODE for Work—and for Life

Many companies use social media to maintain market brand presence or for big data marketing. Those tools generate leads, but what counts for the bottom line are sales not unqualified leads! You need the right tools to manage your relational ROI from qualified leads through completed contract *and referral.*

This is how good free agents drum up new opportunities for themselves. The toolkit your company needs in order to grow is the same toolkit that your employees need in their own lives to survive and thrive in a free agent economy. The processes and behaviors for generating sales are the same for a company team as they are for an individual. Learning CODE is a win for the company and a win for the employee.

Now you know why your employees—not just your sales team—will adopt CODE. There's something in it for them—and for the company. That "something" is a steady pipeline of opportunities that converts predictably to sales. Both your company *and* your employees can use CODE to generate income.

When you explain the economic picture to employees and then present CODE as both the company's and their own survival kit, it's amazing how quickly employees jump on the bandwagon. A light bulb goes off and they get it: no matter what the technology or workflow or product, no matter what individual, company or team, *this is how to convert relationships into business.*

I have never encountered a company that was not already using some derivative of the MAP and YBR in their workflow. The problem is that they need a standardized process to connect the dots and explain how these human-to-human sales should occur. They need a way to deliver this solution and to make it more measurable and predictable across the entire company.

Bottom line? You can adapt your CRM or other existing workflow technologies to these concepts. Or you can use ours.

We believe firmly that in today's world, it's time for the whole sales process to become much easier to manage. And, we believe that everyone's relational contributions to the team should be acknowledged and rewarded. That's why we built 1BLACKBOOK™.

So, whether you opt to go entirely with 1BLACKBOOK™, to use it as a bolt-on to your current system, or to stay solo with whatever technology you've already got, CODE will get everyone aligned and engaged in thinking and behaving differently. CODE creates the relationship-driven culture that you've always wanted your company to thrive on. If you are wondering what the next big wave will be, consider this:

In the merger of technology and human experience, your social currency is your most valuable asset.

Or to quote Louis Columbus in *Forbes*, "Gartner's latest forecasts show that enterprises are realizing the most valuable assets they have are solid, long-term customer relationships. Trust really is the new currency."[12]

---

[12] Columbus, Louis. "Gartner Predicts CRM Will Be a $36 Billion Market by 2017." *Forbes*. 18 Jun. 2013. Web. 16 Dec. 2014.

- Marketing, sales and IT are integrating and companies are struggling to monetize relationships as technology decreases degrees of separation.

- Now every employee—not just sales people—must use their personal and professional relationships to sell themselves and company products. Sales success depends on using who employees know to reach who the company wants to know.

- CODE = Communicate, Organize, Document, Evaluate. It's how to convert relationships to sales.

- Get your team on board by showing what's in it for them. Start with a team of early adapters to secure long-term culture change and revenue results.

- Match every team member to specific sales roles—Prospector, Technical Expert or Closer—according to their capabilities and interests.

- Coordinate the team with simple tools and clear progress goals. Measure efforts with accountability.

- Use two tools: a Marketing Action Plan (MAP) listing everyone you know and want to know and a Yellow-Blue-Red (YBR) color-coded sales pipeline.

- Every company already does this in some form, but they need a consistent way to get every single employee engaged with sales and using their networks to produce measurable, predictable results.

- 1BLACKBOOK.com (or other CODE-friendly technology) will reinforce the rainmaking culture you need and track the ROI of every relationship connected to anyone in your company.

How to Implement Change

Chapter Three: the Psychology of CODE

"All hands on deck!" means everyone—from the top down.

No one wakes up in the morning and plans to fail. No one thinks, "Oh yeah, today is the day I underperform." Business owners want their companies to thrive and make a profit. Employees want to succeed. Nothing feels better than to see a new product or service wildly succeed, to go home at night and say, "I had a hand in that." What could be more rewarding?

So... if everyone wants the company to succeed, why isn't every employee making that happen by nurturing relationships that result in sales? Where's the disconnect?

Let's begin with training. Many employees, especially those who are expected to support sales, underperform because they weren't trained well. Why? Many companies operate without a clear process to identify key roles and responsibilities in relation to sales. Others hire employees without establishing specific performance expectations from the beginning.

When I interview salespeople who lost jobs because they didn't perform well, many tell me their initial training went something like this: "Okay, starting today, you're going to ride with Frank for a few weeks and then read a book on business or receive a set of targets to pursue. We'll review your progress now and then. Welcome aboard!"

In this scenario, management didn't clearly define success. They didn't state any expectations about how to farm core customer accounts. They didn't explain how to hunt for new contacts. The result? They set the employee up to fail.

Individual success determines corporate success. The more every individual employee succeeds at sales, the more the company succeeds.

Often, management finds it easier to identify the symptoms of the problem: "Our salespeople didn't meet their goals." Or, "We lost great talent to the competition." They grab hold of one or two trees and miss the forest.

What's the big picture? Come up with real solutions that make a fundamental difference to your company's sales dynamics. Fully implement an intentional process. Start with where the company and its existing practices currently stand and then deploy every employee to sell. Coordinate their efforts and make sure to hold everyone accountable. Help employees adopt the skills they need for you to reap the rewards of sustainable change.

How does this begin? Shift the company mindset.

It's the Entrepreneurial Way

No one disputes how important customers are to organizations. However, many employees don't possess the mindset to nurture those relationships in strategic ways. They aren't trained to do it, either. Companies typically hired them for a set of technical skills, not to manage relationships. But in the approaching free agent economy, everyone will need to adapt and develop better relationship-building skills. It's vital to the company's success, and to individual security. The company's relationships to their customers are everything. No skill is more important than the ability to consistently cultivate those relationships.

Here's how one company tackled the challenge of changing their employees' mindset. The Stansell Electric Corporation, a third generation company based in Nashville, hired me to implement

CODE. We created a company-wide focus on sales and customer service. Basil Hall, the vice president of Stansell at the time, called out the company's problem:

"Our company did not have a sales culture. We did good work and we expected people to call us to give us more work. But as the market got tighter, suddenly people weren't calling as much. At that point, no one from the company was cultivating relationships intentionally or pursuing targeted opportunities. Those who were out there were using the 'shotgun approach,' talking to lots of people and hoping to get work, but that mostly failed."

I introduced the basic CODE concepts to company leaders. The company president, David Stansell, called together a company-wide meeting. Hall later reported:

"David opened the meeting and said, 'Here's where we are and here's where the market seems to be going. We'd like to get more sales so we can grow, have more projects going on, have our jobs more secured and make more of a profit. How many of you are interested in that?' Everyone raised a hand.

"'Okay, what are you prepared to do to help achieve that?' There was a lot of confusion. People wondered what he meant.

"'We have found a system that will allow us to become more effective in communicating with customers, in building relationships, as well as in recognizing and then pursuing opportunities to work more effectively for those customers. We're not completely transforming what we are already doing every day, but only adding to it. Is there anyone who's not interested or willing to be a part of this?'

"Everyone seemed to be all right with that. So we went ahead and did the [CODE] training with Elizabeth where the idea of everyone acting as a salesperson was introduced.

"After that, we had another meeting. David said, 'Okay, now that you've had the training, are there any questions?' There was a lot of pushback—a lot of, 'Wait a minute. I never said I was a salesman.'

"David said, 'That's true, and you don't have to be. But if you tell me you're not a communicator, then you're probably not going to have a job here because there's no position in this company where we can do our work without being able to communicate with others. All we're asking you to do is learn a different set of tools for communicating, and to use them little by little.'"

David led the change from the top down. Which brings up a very important point: **to successfully shift the mindset, leaders have to spearhead the effort**. Assign every employee a clear role specific to the sales process, and explain how that role works with others to produce measurable results. Then, leaders must take it one critical step further: modeling those roles to the employees.

The Three Roles

Every organization, no matter what its size, uses the three roles of CODE to execute their sales process, whether they realize it or not. Entrepreneurs move through these roles almost subconsciously, often without labeling them. CODE identifies and breaks out these implicit roles by causing the company to make them explicit, intentional and accountable. That way, every employee connects to their assigned role(s) with measurable and specific skills, attitudes and behaviors. Let's go ahead and revisit the roles in this context:

The Prospector

Prospectors develop business or generate leads. They drum up interest in the company's products or services. *Entrepreneurs are natural Prospectors.* They're always excited to talk about their ideas and products. Their livelihoods, and in some cases their life purposes, are tied to what they sell. For them, prospecting is as critical as breathing.

Prospectors are always hunting for new opportunities. And they naturally farm, too, because they depend on past relationships that produced opportunities. The customers in the second group often become core customers, who provide the stable revenue that makes a company fiscally strong while it moves forward and hunts for future business.

Anyone can become a Prospector by hunting or farming—or both. For the whole company to succeed at sales, leaders and employees have to understand and know when to play this role.

I once surveyed a group of CEOs. Every one of them said it was reasonable to expect *every* employee to act as a farmer in order to nurture core customer relationships. Easily said. Not so easily done. How do people from different departments contribute to building a cohesive relationship? Basil Hall said Stansell Electric created a new understanding of how fundamental it is to build customer relationships:

> *"Some of our employees are in front of our customers ten times as much as a salesman. If they are not doing any- thing to secure the customer's relationship, and their loyalty, then we're missing this huge opportunity. All that's required of them is to be friendly and interested. Ask ques- tions like, 'How did we do last time?' 'What else have you got coming?' That has been key. Just those two things."*

Another client, a company president (but not entrepreneurial founder), was a natural introvert, a technical expert and a highly-skilled operations guru. Initially, he felt uncomfortable with the idea of acting in any kind of sales capacity. It wasn't like him to "naturally act like a Prospector."

However, once he learned CODE, he gave himself permission to "start where he was" and consciously prospect for opportunities through his executive network. He effectively "cashed in" his so- cial currency as the leader of this high-profile company. He developed new relationships and called in old favors or referrals from people who trusted and knew him well. He built credibility with other decision-makers. He also effected a complete 180-degree reversal from the way he had viewed himself before.

Eventually, he personally drove a full 50% of his company's new business development. He led through example, and his entire service department rallied behind him. The result? The company was able to avoid the painful layoffs of 19 team members. This win inspired the other reporting departments, and the company began to enjoy a new level of success.

Anyone who connects with customers or prospects to any degree or in any capacity can fulfill this role. Sennheiser, a high-end headphone and speaker manufacturer, sends its *engineers* to trade fairs to talk on the front lines with customers. Why? High-end equipment users focus on quality technology. Who better to answer their questions credibly than engineers? Sure, they are Technical Experts, but at these trade fairs, they change hats and act as Prospectors. They're sharing their knowledge and piquing the attendees' interest in buying Sennheiser headphones.

Everyone can be a Prospector. A shift in mindset empowers them to do it.

The Technical Expert

Technical Experts aid in identifying a prospect's needs, especially when qualifying the scope of work required. Can you provide a specific solution to this customer? How? Does their definition of value align with our definition of price? Technical Experts gauge the answer to these questions and typically provide the product, service or direct value to the customer. In manufacturing, Technical Experts include project managers, account managers, engineers and technicians. In professional services, they appear in the form of architects, lawyers, accountants and marketers. Technical Experts perform the work at hand, but they are equally capable of farming current customers and hunting for new ones.

The Closer

The Closer has the authority and ability to close a deal with a prospect. If you compare the sales force of an organization to a rock band in concert, the Closer would be the lead singer. He or she connects with the crowd, gauges their emotional buy-in and delivers the goods—the full experience. Closers have a very keen understanding of how to manage social currency. They know what people value and consistently demonstrate their ability to deliver that value while building trust.

Companies Must Embrace "All Hands on Deck"

Jiffy Lube has taken its business development effort to a whole new level. They fulfill all three roles of the sales process in an immediate way. Whenever they have a gap in their pipeline, they require their technical staff members to stand outside, waving at traffic while wearing signs that read, "No Wait for Oil Change. Right now!" They are boots-on-the-ground **Prospectors**.

Once a car pulls in, a technician attends to the customer. He asks about the customer's needs (qualifying the job). Then he directs the car into a bay for service (**Technical Expert**). Once the car has been checked, he updates the client on findings, suggests any needed service and states the urgency of that service (**Closer**). At the point of purchase, a staff member provides documentation as a reminder for a future date-of-service (**Post Sale**).

In short, Jiffy Lube gets its technical staff directly involved in generating leads and participating in each critical role. The entire team actively drives business to the company, which is a big change from the days when you'd drive by and notice a number of tech folks smoking behind the building during down time.

I call this "All Hands on Deck." All employees, even those not directly related to business development, sales or marketing, focus on one goal: bringing in new business. *Anyone in the company can engage customers, drive demand and support the organization's sales efforts.* It simply requires a shift in mindset to get employees aligned with how this works.

When I implement CODE with my clients, I first invite employees to "think like entrepreneurs." What must entrepreneurs do to thrive? Prospect. I train employees to think like Prospectors who focus on nurturing relationships critical to the organization. I explain how to be on the lookout for opportunities in every encounter: what to listen for, how to "read the need" in gestures or comments and how to follow up with what they might hear or learn. Next, I instruct them in the role of the Technical Expert and identify what's required of a Closer.

When we're done, everyone in the organization intentionally focuses on nurturing relationships. They do what's required to build trust, ask for help and work together in tighter alignment across the ranks to create new business. They start with focusing on attitudes, skills and behaviors appropriate to practicing roles and responsibilities associated with CODE.

What does this process look like from a company's perspective? GENESYS Systems Integrator Doug Lenny explained what happened at their company:

> "People on my team were operating as their own islands, per se. What the three roles allowed us to do was understand that when an opportunity was identified, we needed to work together to try to get it done. How? We identified that I was the Prospector, that someone else was the Technical Expert and that our departmental leader was the Closer. We recognized that a job was going to require more than one person and that we needed to use the right people at the right stages with the right skills to complete the sale. That's what really helped us."

> "By identifying the roles, we work more as a team now. [The way we approach opportunities] is understanding that, 'I can win this but I need help on this and this and this.' You learn to set the meetings up and work as a team to bring the right people in at the right time. It's not one person anymore."

Before implementing CODE, GENESYS experienced internal dynamics that ran against the strength of its people. Several employees coordinated client services and sold across multiple departments. They weren't always successful. They were slotted into traditional roles. But when each person recognized how his or her strengths could help the sales process, they started working as an effective team for each sale. Each person contributed more value to the process. They also asked for support when they needed it.

As a result, they have had a 20% increase in negotiated work and have experienced one of their most profitable years on record. They are even turning down work. When is the last time your company did that? Solid departmental cross-communication allows them to select work most profitable and appropriate to maximize operational capacity.

Is there a specific formula to deploy the roles of Prospector, Technical Expert and Closer? No. Every organization will do it a bit differently. The roles may be divided among individuals, teams, or divisions. At times, some senior management leaders or principals in larger organizations will take on all three roles. Of course, solo entrepreneurs or small teams take on all three roles daily. They have no other choice.

To effectively engage the three roles, everyone involved needs to be clear about:

- Where each role fits in the sales process.

- How to match the right roles with the right people, according to expectation, skill set or level of authority. (More on this in later chapters.)

Doug Lenny of GENESYS speaks to the point:

"Code impacted the way I look at things. Now, if I need certain technical questions answered that I myself can't address, I bring someone into the project and identify him as my Technical Expert. Or if I have a project that needs

closing but I've spent weeks without getting anywhere, I might need to bring in a Closer."

"Maybe just as important is that understanding the way the roles work makes me feel more appreciated. Just because I may not be strong as a Closer doesn't mean that my abilities as a Technical Expert or Prospector are less valued. The ability to identify the three roles gives everyone a better sense of worth."

Leaders: Get the Party Started

For an organization to implement CODE successfully, company leaders—principals, managers, influencers and decision-makers—must model the behavior I just described. Leaders have to actually eat what's on the plate and not just pass it around for everyone else. This includes:

- Supporting CODE concept training, so that every employee and new hire will have a uniform understanding of the process and its intent.

- Driving demand by fulfilling their own roles as Prospector, Technical Expert and/or Closer.

- Holding themselves and every other employee accountable to their committed role(s) in the process.

- Encouraging people to embrace the learning curve by describing what works and what doesn't and therefore engaging cross-training between junior- and senior-level talent.

Leaders need to engage the process as much as they hold others accountable to it. Employees look to their leaders to set company standards, especially when it involves changing the company culture. It's a question of follow-through: Can those same leaders that implemented CODE model it for their employees by consistently committing themselves to the essential progress reporting?

For those accustomed to "doing their own thing" or operating a company without a standardized sales process, it can be challenging at first to systematize an organization's sales efforts.

Some managers hold their teams accountable while avoiding accountability themselves. This is an untenable double standard. If this happens, the process loses traction. Life reverts to the haphazard way the sales process functioned before.

Look at this problem through the prism of weight loss. People want to lose weight, but 75% fail. Why? Assuming no medical problem, people know how important it is to exercise and eat right. But making the attitude and behavioral changes is another matter entirely. Everything from self-reflection to adopting new eating and exercise habits eludes them. It's outside their comfort zone, and they don't want to be accountable.

Similarly, leaders may *want* to shift to a company-wide focus on sales. They might even sign off on adopting CODE. However, if they lack the sincere commitment to hold themselves or others accountable to the process, the team interprets it as a low priority. It's not what management says that matters; it's what they *do*. Remember what Yoda said in *Star Wars*? "There is no 'try'. There is only 'do.'" As David Kirkpatrick wrote in a 2011 *Forbes.com* article:

> *"In today's brave new business world, companies and leaders will have to show authenticity, fairness, transparency and good faith. If they don't, customers and employees may come to distrust them, to potentially disastrous effect. Customers who don't like a product can quickly broadcast their disapproval. Prospective employees don't have to take your word for what life is like at your company—they can find out from people who already work there."*[13]

---

[13] Kirkpatrick, David. "Social Power And The Coming Corporate Revolution." *Forbes.com.* 7 Sept. 2011. Web. 1 Oct. 2014.

When leaders commit *themselves* to the new process, they create the energy to change the company mindset. A few good questions to ask before you begin:

- Are leaders and team members willing to try new roles and responsibilities? What is their next step if that challenges everyone to expand his or her communication skills?

- What happens if the company enjoys sales success while encountering operational capacity issues? Will commitment to the new system lag?

- How do leaders demonstrate the discipline and commitment required to continually feed the prospect pipeline—in good times and bad?

- Are leaders willing to address organizational apathy by moving outside their individual comfort zones?

Bottom line: if the leadership remains committed, the rest of the company will follow.

Companies Must Leverage the Relational Value of the Human Brand

Here's another pivotal piece to adopting a new company mindset: acknowledging the power of the "Human Brand." The human brand deeply impacts a company's reputation due to the first rule of business: **People do business with people they like.**

The customer is the lifeblood of all organizations. While this sounds obvious, companies often behave with a disconnect between what they say and what they actually do. They might want to protect and expand the existing customer base. Then they approach it passively. Or, they don't reach out to customers at all. They have great intentions, but don't convert that to action. Employees' actions and communications affirm the true core values of an organization—whether they want it to or not.

The human brand colors customer expectations during any transaction or engagement with an organization. Customers often associate a name or face with a company. They think about how the company will treat them, how well the company will manage their expectations, how attuned and responsive the employees will be to their needs and how much they'll enjoy doing business with that company.

The "C" in CODE represents *intentional* communication. At the most fundamental level, the human brand of an organization communicates the values and customer promises associated with it.

Here's an illustration of this idea. A colleague of mine went to Las Vegas on vacation. She was unsure where to stay and decided to check out a few resorts. When she stopped at the Wynn Resort, a janitor was vacuuming the lobby carpet. When he spotted her, he turned off the machine, walked over, introduced himself, shook her hand and asked if he could help her. On the spot, she decided to stay there. She figured if the janitor embodied that kind of service, the rest of the staff would be phenomenal. It wasn't the janitor's job to roll out the welcome mat. But when he did, he made an instant sale for his employer and a lasting brand impression on the customer.

Human brands are not static or based on vague abstracts, corporate names or symbols. They embody the promise behind a customer's dynamic experience during any transaction, large or small. Consider this an extension of the company mission statement—and nothing less.

This is why organizations need to make a *conscious effort* to identify the values that will be delivered through the attitudes and behaviors of their employees. A human brand may translate to something quite basic, like identifying a few universally positive human traits and asking employees to consciously apply them whenever engaging customers, vendors—or each other: "More and more, brands are gaining traction by embracing qualities like honesty, kindness, and simply… a sense of humor."[14]

I introduced a tagline to a client, City Wide Maintenance. They offer premium-level janitorial services. The company wanted its people to cross-sell their services, to avoid simply competing on price. The slogan I suggested? "We aren't Janitors; we're Great Managers!" The idea was for the janitors to take more of an ownership stake in the clients' larger needs, such as window cleaning, parking lot stripping, or even event management. When they took the initiative to think like managers, they built trust. Then they moved into cross-selling other, less price-sensitive services. Their new mindset, reflected by a single slogan, helped City Wide Maintenance grow from seven to 24 franchise locations throughout the U.S.

There are very basic, practical ways employees can fulfill the promise of their human brand. They can take the initiative when faced with a customer issue. Don't pass the problem along to someone else. Ask how someone is doing—a customer, a vendor, a colleague—for no other reason than just to ask. As GENESYS Systems Integrator sales manager Roger Hagen noted,

> "Because of CODE, we concentrate much more on relationships throughout our company. Our accounts payable people are a good example. They frequently interact with customers in stressful situations. But when they've made a good impression and a good personal connection with that customer, they've done a good job. As a company, we encourage everyone to reinforce relationships—to reinforce the brand with everyone they talk to."

Sales always begins with the intentional act of building quality relationships.

---

[14] Boyd, E.B. "For Brands, Being Human Is The New Black." *Fast Company*. 29 Aug. 2011. Web. 12 Oct. 2014.

- Everyone can contribute to the sales effort—not just those in sales.

- Consider these two activities: farming existing customers and hunting for new ones. Identify who in your organization would make good farmers and hunters.

- Invite employees to consider this initiative and explain what's in it for them in light of key trends (free agent economy).

- Talk to each employee about the value of acting like an entrepreneur. Invite them to consider how "thinking like a rainmaker" might help their children or family to uncover new opportunities in their relational networks.

- Assign each participating employee a role— Prospector, Technical Expert or Closer. Choose a role that matches their abilities so they can fulfill their individual responsibility to company sales.

- Company leaders must spearhead the shift in company mindset by holding themselves personally accountable to the new sales process. They must model the very practices they expect their employees to adopt.

- Simply put, relationships are the lifeblood of all organizations.

- Success requires clear communication (the "C" in CODE).

- Identify specific values you want your employees to communicate to customers in order to create or fortify your human brand.

Chapter Four: First Steps to Implementation

"We know what we want to be doing, but we're just not doing it."

The Need for a Common Language

The CODE system is like a car engine, which requires multiple components to work together as a unit in order to function ideally. An engine depends on the driver to operate the car. Likewise, CODE depends on its practitioners to drive the sales process more effectively and predictably. When everyone in an organization can identify the moving parts associated with the sales process and how those elements fit together, they become better drivers of demand.

CODE revolves around clear communication between customers, salespeople and other employees. Clear communication depends on having a simple, standardized vocabulary. Anyone who has ever dealt with misunderstandings during a sales meeting can appreciate how much a standard vocabulary makes a remarkable difference for all involved.

Take the most overused term in sales: the "hot lead." What goes through your mind when you consider that phrase? By whose standard is it hot? The salesperson's? The company's? What does "hot" mean? That the sale is all but in the bag? *What?* And what about the two key questions that might be asked if a "hot lead" is presented: Is the opportunity funded? Has it been adequately qualified *before* investing internal resources to pursue it further?

That's a lot of guesswork for a term synonymous with successful selling. It's exactly the reason why I emphasize a simple, standardized vocabulary in the CODE process. Without clearly defining where a lead falls within the sales process, it's hard to figure out the best next steps to move it forward. This leads to wasted revenue, time and effort. Predictable sales depend on a common vocabulary.

CODE precisely defines the sales process and the roles required to execute that process. An organization can easily adapt these definitions to their specific needs. However, the primary goal is for everyone to clearly understand and use the definitions common to all.

Going forward, we'll take a closer look at the elements of CODE, how they fit together, and how to take steps to apply them in *any* sales system.

Let's first revisit the **C-O-D-E** acronym itself and then consider how you can get started with applying CODE.

"C" (Intentional) Communication

An organization's human brand communicates the values and promises the customer associates with the company. Do your employees understand how their behaviors, attitudes and skill sets align with your mission? Clear communication helps drive accountability and results.

"O" Organization

Generally, management organizes the new sales process by assigning roles. They determine which team members or individuals will engage in a particular aspect of CODE. For example, those most often in direct communication with customers, such as Account Management or Project Managers, can actively support the sales process as Prospectors. Their jobs position them to farm for new leads, referrals or information. Others will be more involved in the entire CODE process and its related tools: sales teams, marketing people, technicians, engineers, and management.

If you want your company to implement CODE, assign the roles of Prospectors, Technical Experts and Closers. The next step is to assign the responsibilities of farming and hunting. After that, you'll create a targeted relational MAP and YBR sales pipeline. Open for discussion the question, "Who is the best Prospector, Technical Expert and Closer in this situation?" Give each person a primary role that matches talents and job descriptions. Who is the most natural person to nurture relationships with core customers?

I say the same thing to every leader with which I consult: Don't over think this process. (If you still need help figuring out how to assign roles for your organization, refer to the Implementation Tips at the back of this book.) I also remind them of a few other major considerations:

- Almost everyone can be responsible for farming or taking care of core customers (all hands on deck).

- Technical experts may naturally push back.

- Time is your long-term ally. It will help you sort out who should be involved and how. (It usually becomes obvious, even if you may not have identified someone initially.)

After you've assigned roles, drive your company to organized accountability by using the MAP and YBR to guide the process.

"D" Documentation

Ensure a paperwork trail or system to transform a largely intuitive process into one that can be monitored, followed, and evaluated. The MAP kicks off the process. To engage, you need a tracking system like 1BLACKBOOK™ or another CRM that gives a clear picture of what each person in the organization is contributing to the actual sales in process *today*. Just like any communication, documentation needs to be simple, uniform and easily understood.

"E" Evaluation

One of the most important tasks in implementing CODE is the progress meeting that team leaders spearhead. That's where employees report on progress, review their "scorecards" and identify next steps based on results recorded on the MAP and YBR. I recommend weekly meetings to check that all parts are in place and operating at capacity.

In thinking about evaluation, emphasize accountability. In fact, underline it. For CODE to succeed, company leaders attend these meetings to:

- Set an example for employee buy-in.

- Keep the meetings focused and on track.

- Encourage senior-level and junior-level people to learn from each other and cross-train.

We'll focus a lot on documentation and evaluation in the upcoming chapters.

- You need a common sales language to hold your employees accountable to specific, measurable goals.

- "C" Communicate your company values to your employees as you help them focus on nurturing the relationships important to farming and hunting.

- "O" Organize your entire company to be familiar with CODE training, tools and reporting processes.

- "D" Document your organization's relationship inventory (both actual and desired) on the MAP—a comprehensive list of people. Capture the results of farming and hunting on the YBR—a running list of current opportunities or projects.

- "E" Evaluate your team's outcomes in your regular progress meetings.

Chapter Five: Develop the Marketing Action Plan (MAP)

"We've always tried to stay away from making cold calls. Our best sales have come from being connected by some-one who's already a trusted supplier for a company or by someone who has some kind of relationship with us. [Our goal] is to be introduced by someone who has a connection with the company or from some kind of referral."
—*Roger Hagen, GENESYS Systems Integrator*

We all agree that referrals are the best sources to generate leads. While referrals are key to sustainable growth, however, organi-zations must be more proactive in protecting the loyalty of their current customers in this new, hyperconnected economy. An over-dependency on referrals and organic growth does not guar-antee success. Which leads to the million-dollar question: how can organizations creatively leverage current relationships while continuing to work towards securing new ones?

In late 2011, Facebook reported that each of us currently oper-ates at 4.74 degrees of separation.[15] Not long ago (say, before Facebook exploded in 2006), it was 6 degrees of separation. That means that you and I are four or five direct contacts from meet-

---

[15] Backstrom, Lars. "Anatomy of Facebook." *Facebook Data Science.* Facebook. 21 Nov. 2011. Web. 1 Oct. 2014.

ing or doing business with any person or client *in the world.* Our opportunities are exploding, while at the same time, our circles of connectivity are becoming tighter and tighter. This is why organizations must learn how to tap their social currency within their existing networks. It's just simple math, really: If you don't do it, your competition will.

Welcome to the primary purpose of the Marketing Action Plan (MAP): to intentionally leverage your relational networks to win new business.

The CODE MAP provides the means for an organization to tap into and proactively manage and mine their relationships and social contacts. A company's long-term sustainability depends on it. Identifying key contacts and centrally organizing them enables leaders to become more aggressive and intentional about how they manage those contacts.

The MAP centralizes them, and creates a place for entire teams or divisions to update and systematically evaluate relationships. Unlike a CRM, which often functions as an unwieldy address book, the purpose of a MAP is to manage the depth and ROI of relationships—both existing and those you wish you had. It's a simple, comprehensive list of who you know and who you want to know.

Begin with "Who You Know"

The average organization's relational assets are spread all over the place: LinkedIn, individual employee email lists in places like Outlook or Constant Contact, Christmas lists, and contacts for particular divisions or departments—local, regional or international. Everyone seems to have a list. Whether a company is a family-owned business with only a handful of employees or is enterprise-sized with tens of thousands, the idea in creating the MAP is the same: to make a centralized relational inventory that meticulously identifies every key relationship in the organization.

Most organizations have no system for consolidating their relational networks, nor a systematic way to share intelligence or manage those relationships among individual salespeople or divisions. However, industry leaders are waking up. They are realizing they must do this to remain competitive.

One publicly traded company hired me to help address this problem. Their organization included 16 individual firms and $4 billion market capitalization. Their management wanted to consolidate their relational inventory into a MAP under the CODE system. Why? So they could be more strategic about how they managed their relationships in order to meet their short- and long-term goals.

One primary difference between the traditional approaches to sales and business development and the CODE process is that the former focuses on sales outcomes alone. CODE switches the focus to the *relationships* connected to the sales. They wanted to maintain and grow long-term relationships. Today, a customer you thought was loyal can switch companies in the tap of an iPhone app. Don't let that happen. Relationship-building means *everything*.

Standard marketing plans identify companies within industries as targets. However, they rarely take the next critical step: to identify and rank the human-to-human relationships your employees build with people at those target companies. Consequently, there's a missing accountability link between the marketing "plan" and the day-to-day activities of salespeople and business development teams. The MAP provides that crucial missing link.

Put the Map Together

Let's develop the MAP. First, itemize all contacts into two categories: "Who you know" and "Who you want or need to know." Draw from sources like:

- **Core customers:** repeat clients whose business has provided significant sales (and who should be actively maintained by a company's employees through farming efforts).

- **Important vendor/suppliers:** people who owe favors and may serve as good sources for introductions.

- **Strategic partnerships:** other organizations that offer important professional relationships and value.

- **Industry peers.**

- **Extended corporate relationships:** personal friends, family and acquaintances.

Document each relationship on the map. Include the usual contact information (name, telephone numbers, email and physical addresses). Now go beyond that. Document the relationship-based information you have on that contact. Include:

- Current position

- Past positions with respective employers

- His or her important clients, peers, coworkers, etc. (Who does he or she know?)

- Organizational stakeholders the contact has a relationship with or reports to

Feeling overwhelmed? Start with a basic list of core customers. I move my clients out of procrastinating on this task by asking, "When was the last time you were in front of your top 25 customers?" For one client, this top 25 starting point jump-started the larger MAP-building effort. Take it one small bite at a time to overcome any sense of organizational apathy.

Add "Who You Want to Know" to the MAP

Every organization has the same challenge: to find new customers and new opportunities. Leaders try new ideas, but success varies wildly. How do you target those new customers? Through trade shows? Sponsoring golf tournaments? Building better brand awareness? Social networking or social media marketing?

Here's the problem with every one of those approaches: unless they offer a way to measurably determine the relational and revenue outcome, they end up eating up huge investments of time, capital or both, while lacking precision and focus. They're often inexact, expensive and impossible to measure, and therefore unpredictable. GENESYS Systems Integrator's Doug Lenny documented what happened when they started working with the CODE MAP:

> "We did well in the past when we had repeat customers— we always did good work with those customers—but we didn't really know how to go out and find new customers. Everybody has a list of who they've done business with, but the MAP is a tool that really opens your eyes of how to effectively go in and use that list to start reconnecting with those contacts.

> "This list shows you where to farm, but you also need to diversify and find new companies to add to that list. In real life, you can only effectively farm a field so long before you use up all the resources there. You need to add some nitrogen or at least let the field rest for a bit. In the meantime, you have to go out and hunt every now and then; you have to bring in new opportunities and new players."

Next question: who do you *want* to know? Answering that will help your organization define what it wants to achieve beyond the vague mission of 'more sales.' The answer will reflect your organization's overall strategy and will focus your motivation as you go forward.

Use the MAP to evaluate both the strength and the relative cross-sell opportunities that the company may be missing, especially in large or national accounts. Look for new strategic business plans or market opportunities to surface. When you work the current list of "who we know" within key accounts, you'll see patterns emerge that are worthy of further exploration.

This creates the opportunity for your organization to stretch and improve on current practices. You can set a new and highly actionable standard. The MAP enables leaders and team members to have a frank discussion about where things stand, as well as to project where they could be and how to get there.

Compiling the List of Who You Want to Know

The task of compiling this list will vary from one organization to another, depending on size, leadership style and general culture. But the goal is the same: to determine what new relationships may most likely lead to new opportunities. Right now, social networks suggest "who you may know," but for strategic selling practices, there's a major difference between who you *may* know and *who you want to know.* The goal of the MAP's list is to really think about the types of decision makers—by title, industry or specialty—that make the most sense for you to pursue. David Price, former president of Wachter Electric, noted:

> "To identify our MAP targets, we met as a team and determined what market segments we felt had the potential to grow. After picking the industries, we defined what types of companies in those industries we needed to focus on, such as size. Then we identified specific companies that geographically matched our profile and used them to create our list. Finally, we assigned our sales guys to strategically hunt for opportunities in those companies."

Initially, the targets may not include specific individuals. Even so, the ultimate goal is to find a way to shrink down your degrees of separation from a titled person in the company, preferably a decision-maker. Until your team can identify a specific person, list a target company as a "broad target." Tools such as Jigsaw or LinkedIn are solid resources for identifying specific company targets, as both offer free basic services and basic search capabilities. Then, as GENESYS' Doug Lenny points out:

> "The goal is to find out who has veto power. Someone may give us great information on an opportunity, but it's important to know who the actual decision-makers are (in

our case, people capable of issuing a purchase order). By establishing who that is via internal communications and adding this data to their names to the MAP, it can make a real difference when it's time to close the project. We already know who we need to be having certain conversations with [to close]. The MAP really helps you figure out who the critical people are in the company and how an organization works."

Creating the initial list of contacts requires an investment of time. But it's time well-invested. You know you've done your job well when both the MAP contacts and any relevant information about them are readily accessible to Prospectors and Closers. Every other person connected to the sales opportunities with that contact should be able to track and monitor details of the relationship. That way, your team can coordinate how they communicate with specific prospects.

David Price also said that the MAP "lets us know where we stand in terms of [a contact's] loyalty to us and in their willingness to offer us work over time. We need to communicate the value we add and know that they see that value."

Create a great MAP. With a true inventory of the organization's social currency, you'll know where to invest your time and effort to grow.

Ranking Relationships / Quantifying Their Value

Quantify each relationship. Prioritize your prospecting efforts by assigning each name on the MAP a rank from 1 to 5. Anyone referring to the MAP can more accurately determine what action to take to nurture the relationship forward in a measurable way. Again, the relational ranking system works like this:

1 = Doesn't know you.

2 = Knows you, but has never given you business.

3 = You have been shortlisted for work, but there is competition.

4 = You are a single source for work. The contact has shown or expressed loyalty to you.

5 = The contact refers other customers to you.

Depending on the features of your organization's technology, add notes wherever possible to help identify exactly how a contact first became available to the company (and through whom). Add the date and subject of the organization's last contact with that person. Many of my clients add a (+) sign to contacts who have produced referrals and a (-) to any relationships with a history of problems associated with the account. You'll find it very helpful to have that information on the MAP, especially in cases that call for extra sensitivity. If you are using 1BLACKBOOK™, you'll find similar tools readily accessible on your electronic MAP.

Suppose your MAP fills up with hundreds or thousands of contacts—a fairly likely scenario. Where should Prospectors begin?

The lowest hanging fruit on the revenue tree—the easiest to pluck—should be produced by farming your organization's core customer base. These are the relationships ranked "3," "4" or "5" on the MAP. Focus your initial farming efforts here because the probability of selling to a new prospect is only 5-20%, but the probability of selling to an existing customer is 60-70%.[16]

Relationships ranked 3's, 4's and 5's are the easiest to impact quickly. They will give you immediate traction and reward for being proactive with your new system of using CODE. Encourage quality 'face time' between your team and theirs as you inquire after more work and/or referrals. It is all about relationship; people do business with people they like.

Listing all contacts is only the first step. Once listed, Prospectors and those who manage the effort select a few names per week to

---

[16] Farris, Paul W., Neil T. Bendle, Phillip E. Pfeifer, and David J. Reibstein. *Marketing Metrics: The Definitive Guide to Measuring Marketing Performance.* 2nd ed. Upper Saddle River, N.J.: FT, 2010.

assign to those participating in farming or hunting efforts. Prospectors call these targets "Weekly Whites." From people (Whites) come potential sales (Yellows, Blues and Reds). Those opportunities eventually result in 'yes' or 'no' decisions to purchase and lead to post-sales efforts to keep growing the relationship (Greens).

Later, I'll focus specifically on the process of assigning Whites and progress reporting. Here's the point for right now: Whites are lifted from the MAP and assigned to individual Prospectors for farming or hunting efforts.

Your MAP outlines the parameters of your relational game plan. It allows your team access to information on the strategic relationships they need to personally develop right now. All relationships are built on trust, and that trust precedes a transaction. By directing your team to build relationships, you are directing them to lay the foundation for future sales opportunities.

Update the MAP and Keep a Scorecard

Some organizations review their company MAP monthly. Others review it quarterly. Those responsible for CODE implementation are in charge of maintaining and updating the MAP.

Whatever your situation, regular reviews (including taking the time to rank contacts) are crucial. They provide clear indicators of progress for the sales and marketing teams. Over time, you'll see how targeted efforts result in the movement of 1's to 2's and 2's to 3's, and so on. New priorities will emerge. Relationships will drive company strategy.

The relational ROI can be easily monitored over time as rankings improve. Keep and maintain a running scorecard of how your team is developing relationships. How many targeted Weekly Whites are eventually producing opportunities that close (Greens)? Etc.

- Create a Marketing Action Plan (MAP), which is a relational inventory list of all your of company's and employees' relevant relational assets.

- Include not only the relationships you have, but also the relationships you want. Specify individual people wherever possible.

- Rank the relationships' current value on a 1 to 5 scale. Ones don't know you. Twos know you, but have never given you business. Threes have given you some business or included you on their shortlist, but there's competition. Fours single source to you out of loyalty. Fives take action by generating referrals.

- Use the MAP to assign your Prospectors specific targets for relational and business development. Trust precedes transaction, so build relationships based on trust.

- Don't over-complicate it. Start with a list of top 25 customers and rank them. From here, generate White lists.

- Update the MAP on a regular, scheduled basis.

- Measure the progress in moving 4's to 5's, etc. Use that measurement to hold your marketing and sales teams accountable to your quarterly relational goals.

- You can display your measurable progress with a regularly updated company or individual scorecard. This running total summarizes activity (such as weekly new Yellows, Blues or Reds by department) and success rates.

Chapter Six: Convert to Yellow-Blue-Red (YBR)

The YBR illustrates the life force of an organization: it's the sales pipeline. All current opportunities are color-coded depending on status. In short, the YBR offers a detailed understanding of where the organization stands in terms of each given sales opportunity at any given moment.

Most organizations work from a colorless standard spreadsheet that lists all opportunities in play. Sound familiar? Some also assign a hot-warm-cold ranking or a probability-to-close ranking. I've never seen a universal system that clearly defines behaviors to move opportunities forward at each stage of the process. I designed the YBR pipeline and its color codes to do just that.

In this chapter, we'll discuss in more depth why companies benefit from using a universal sales language. I'll explain how the YBR works, and go into detail about the three colors associated with opportunities in the sales pipeline—Yellows, Blues and Reds—as well as the post-sales phase: Greens.

A Common Language: the Four Phases and Three Roles

If you want to improve how different parties communicate with each other, standardize the terminology they use. When everyone agrees on the definitions of key terms, they communicate more clearly about where things stand, what they are about to do, and what they expect others to do next. In sales, standardizing terms helps avoid cases of missed, stalled or even lost opportunities.

The color-coded YBR uses a standard set of definitions that communicates information clearly to the team about the status of a potential sale. The colors define the position of each opportunity in the sales process. Team members can prioritize and communicate the next steps to move the opportunity forward.

Here's a deeper look at the Four Phases and how each of the Three Roles engages with the opportunity pipeline, in CODE terminology with color-coding added:

Phase One: Converting White relationships to Yellow opportunities. Prospectors generate interest in the organization's solutions by hunting or farming. Prospectors use the organization's MAP and list of White contacts to uncover potential opportunities. When the Prospector identifies a confirmed opportunity, he or she enters it into the YBR pipeline as a Yellow.

Phase Two: Converting Yellows into Blues. Now that you know the prospect has a budget and a timeline and is therefore serious about purchasing a solution, set up a time to meet. Once the prospect agrees to meet to discuss the opportunity in detail, reclassify it as a Blue. A Prospector or Technical Expert then works to qualify the project to determine if it's an appropriate match.

Phase Three: When the prospect requests a proposal, bid or RFQ, the Blue opportunity converts to Red. A designated Closer makes the sales pitch, addresses any remaining concerns or final negotiations while driving the sale to a close.

Phase Four: The Prospector or Closer follows up with the prospect, regardless of whether or not the prospect bought the solution. This solidifies the relationship as a potential place to hunt and farm in the future. Opportunities are moved off the YBR opportunity pipeline and color-coded Green. Greens offer a scorecard view of opportunities won, lost or "killed" (died for reasons not associated with sales). Greens are people who have made a yes or no decision. These relationships are "evergreen" as they rotate back to the MAP and are ranked appropriately.

Remember one of CODE's core principles: opportunities begin with actual relationships that the organization must maintain and develop throughout the entire process—and beyond. When a company uses a MAP and YBR, they connect the entire team to the company's growing relationship with the prospect. GENESYS System Integrator's Roger Hagen points out:

> "The YBR was pretty simple for us because it already mirrored our process. All we had to do was classify things into colors. But what the color-coding really did was help us all get clarity on where these opportunities were in the sales cycle. Once we got the sales people arguing about definitions of Yellow or determining what was a Blue, it gave them more clarity in terms of what an opportunity was going to require moving forward."

When you are ready to implement and use the MAP and the YBR, everyone operating under CODE should be able to clearly identify an opportunity, know which color to label it, and be able to discuss with others the next steps appropriate to engage and move the opportunity forward.

This might surprise you, but I always recommend *slowing down* while you implement the YBR system, as employees often have a tendency to misclassify opportunities. A Yellow might really be a Blue, or a Blue might really be a Red. Everyone on the team has to be crystal clear about which color to label each opportunity, because the colors tell everyone else what to do next. The colors coordinate the entire team's relational workflow.

Take the time to review the colors until every team member understands the YBR system well enough to use, and then explain to new hires. If management isn't careful about how to correctly apply the colors, the team will miscommunicate about where opportunities stand, the experience will feel disorganized, and relationships with customers can suffer.

Some people may need more time than others to clearly understand how to apply the color's definitions on a case-by-case basis, especially those employees most resistant to change. But be encouraged: often those most resistant to a new system become its biggest defenders once they adjust to using it.

Yellows

Yellows are opportunities that Prospectors have identified in the lead generation phase. They are 'yellow' because they are 'golden opportunities.' However, no one on the team has yet defined in precise detail the exact solution or specific needs. It's a stage where prospects signal interest in *something* but have a low sense of urgency to move forward.

Some characteristics of Yellows:

- The Prospect is gathering information

- No firm timeline(s) or project scope has been established (low urgency)

- There is funding or budget allocation for the project or opportunity being discussed

- There are few specifications; the prospect may not be clear about details

Warning! Many people make the error of relegating these opportunities to the back burner because the prospect "isn't serious yet." Or they think the opportunity isn't urgent enough to take the time to develop a relationship.

The reality? This is an ideal time for a Prospector to develop a relationship. Do so even *before* an opportunity looks serious, so that as the opportunity develops, you are positioned as the preferred vendor. By working toward this end goal early on, the Prospector can influence issues like vendor preferences and project scope, and maybe even eliminate competition by influencing details associated with an RFP (request for proposal).

Yellows don't call for in-depth action. They do require relatively consistent contact so that when a prospect is ready to accept a meeting (move to blue), they already have an established relationship with you. Some preliminary qualifications you can make:

- Is the opportunity a good fit?

- Is there potential for the organization to add value?

- Does the organization's notion of price correspond to our definition of value?

- Is there a possibility that the project may overwhelm our organization's resources; i.e., do we have adequate capacity?

How does it work well? GENESYS Systems Integrator's Doug Lenny lays it out:

"What is most significant that we have found in CODE, is an emphasis on talking with customers upfront: setting clear expectations about what they, and we, are looking for. Before CODE, we usually just kicked open the door and rushed in. Before we knew it, we were quoting [a project] and investing a lot of company time before we were sure what it was about and had some basic questions answered. Now, we have early conversations to see whether a project is actually plausible and is something we really want to do in the first place."

Blues

Opportunities convert to Blue when the interested party is willing to take a meeting to further discuss. For certain companies, estimates may be generated during the Blue phase. Once a request to meet about a legit opportunity is scheduled, many technical experts have a natural desire to accelerate the process toward a close.

What you need to do is the opposite. Slow down, cool off, and establish mutual respect by honestly assessing whether the opportunity is a good fit for all sides. We label opportunities at this stage 'blue', because blue is a cool color. It reminds you to *cool down*, not ramp up.

On the other hand, some salespeople don't engage assertively with prospects until they're ready to request a proposal, bid, or estimate (when the opportunities are Reds). Both extremes are mistakes. By color-coding your opportunities, your entire team manages their own behaviors and expectations for each stage. That enables your team to effectively manage the prospect's expectations, too. No one likes to be blindsided by a sudden, aggressive sales pitch.

The primary action required for Blues is to meet with the prospect and thoroughly qualify the opportunity. Is the opportunity and your company's solutions a solid match? As Doug Lenny explains:

> "I don't want a client comparing apples to apples. My solution to Line Item 123 is typically going to be different from other bidders' and I want the client to understand that. If they're doing a rebuild of their production line, I'm not just going to bid the job off of their specifications. I'm going to spend time with them on-site at their plant to understand what really needs to be done. We're going to review all the problems and factors, then discuss what our company thinks needs to be done and what doesn't need to be done."

> "When we're finished, we're not bidding on the same project everyone else has bid on. It's, 'Here's a recap of our discussion. This is what you say you want done, here's the additional information I owe you by Friday, here's the additional pricing you'll need to accomplish the solution we've agreed on, and here's what's going to happen when we do the project for you.' And the customer is saying to their team, 'Okay, GENESYS says we're going to take that out. They're going to move it over here and do this with it.'

"By being there, we've come up with new ideas and better ways to do what they want done, but we can't do that without taking the extra time to strengthen the relationship with the customer, solidifying understandings, demonstrating the value we bring to the table."

Qualify the opportunity with the Eight Qualifying Questions, which we'll examine in chapter eight.

Reds

It's easy to define Reds. They are opportunities that have requested a bid, estimate or proposal. A decision to buy—or not—is imminent. These opportunities are "red-hot" and fast moving. They demand immediate attention.

The two most important criteria for classifying opportunities as Red:

- Financing and a timeline for decision making are in place

- Prospects have requested a bid, estimate, proposal or RFQ

At this stage, it's time for your Closer to move in to negotiate and close the deal with the decision maker, or the person with the power to issue a purchase order.

Beyond the YBR: Greens—Keeping Score

Too often, the fourth phase of the sales process is entirely overlooked. Once you've closed a deal, there's a moment of celebration, and then the salespeople tend to move on to the next big thing. But wait a second! How did we do, *really?* Take the time to evaluate the conditions associated with these won (or lost) opportunities. That way, you'll keep the organization's scorecard current. What's working? What's not? How did we close it? Why did we lose the opportunity during or after our close?

You need to know. So does everyone else connected to the sales effort. This is how you improve your team's efforts over time, and how you improve your customer relationships as well.

When a Red opportunity comes to a final decision—Yes or No— it converts to Green and your team assigns it one of three categories: Won, Lost or Killed.

The importance of tracking wins and losses might be obvious. But too often, "killed" opportunities aren't added into the mix. They may have been solid opportunities that suddenly lost funding. Or, the company may have been deemed an unsatisfactory match (for issues beyond immediate control). It's important to record this information, since the relationship may still be in play even though the particular opportunity is not.

Here's an example from the heights of the filmmaking world. Through the late 1990s and the early 2000s, PIXAR and Disney were at war because PIXAR's state-of-the-art animation movies were making Disney irrelevant in a hurry. Disney tried several times to acquire PIXAR, then its creative team and post-production facilities in separate deals, but never succeeded. It didn't help that PIXAR's CEO, the late Steve Jobs, and Disney's Michael Eisner disliked each other intensely.

However, despite a few acrimonious moments, they maintained the relationship. Disney worked out a way to contribute to PIXAR's distribution—something PIXAR needed. Then, they partnered up a little more closely. Finally, when Bob Iger replaced Eisner as CEO of Disney, he and Jobs green-lighted a merger. In 2006, PIXAR became part of Disney. Now, the new and repurposed Walt Disney Animation Studios is an animation juggernaut, the standard-bearer for animated features in the 21st century—just as Disney once owned cartoon animation innovation for decades.

Categorically, when Greens are put into won, lost or killed columns, they summarize overall performance on an ongoing basis. Still, Greens represent more than opportunities. They represent evergreen relationships established during the sales process. At the end of the sales process, your team administrator lifts the names of people associated with the opportunity and updates their relationship rating status on the MAP. (Note: There are some opportunities that an organization will decide not to pursue again under any circumstances. The team may take these opportunities and relationships out of the sales process entirely. However, given the rate of employee turnover due to the contractor-based workforce, I do not recommend name removal.)

Organizing the YBR: Practical Considerations

Most organizations already work from a spreadsheet or pipeline to monitor progress. You can use this "starter list" as a basis for creating the YBR. If no core list exists, document every opportunity your team is aware of or pursuing to populate the initial YBR. That includes information now lodged squarely in the minds of your salespeople (yellows).

Typically, in organizations with multiple divisions, each division will use its own YBR. While it's possible to translate divisional YBRs into one master YBR, I usually advise caution in doing this on a spreadsheet, because it can quickly get too unwieldy. It can be a challenge to update properly, and ends up becoming irrelevant to those contributing to the sales effort. With our technology 1BLACKBOOK™, you have the option to organize your different teams' YBRs in a way that makes sense for your company's overall organization.

Service Calls

If the organization has a sales process that typically converts inbound calls to a Red within one or two actions (i.e., Yellow opportunities that go straight to Red), consider integrating YBRs. This could apply to service departments or field personnel who respond directly to inquiries. In such instances, management will want to determine the most appropriate leads to add to the YBR.

For example, one electrical service group had dozens of people working on inbound service calls, which included small projects under $25K. They felt it too cumbersome to ask their people to document all leads, and decided to document and track on their YBR only the projects over $25K.

If there is any question, I encourage management to ask their people to present what they have already been documenting (existing CRM, bid log, estimating log, pending proposal list). This will reveal internal priorities and organic systems of information management. Move forward from your organic systems, tweaking them to reflect ideas associated with the MAP and YBR.

For some organizations, most often the very large or very small, a central YBR does have merit. It will chronicle the total value of the organization's pipeline and help to establish a gauge for the organization's position in terms of operational capacity. My clients have also used it to defend credit worthiness and bonding capacity. Central and divisional YBRs graphically communicate the same thing: how quickly and how often opportunities convert to business (Yellows to Blues, Blues to Reds, and Reds to Greens). Over time, historical data on the YBR becomes an excellent financial predictor for the company.

Companies should incorporate **Scorecards** to capture the percent of Yellows, Blues and Reds that met or exceeded profit margin goals. 1BLACKBOOK™ updates Scorecards automatically so you can measure progress individually, divisionally and across the company.

Organizing the Team

Before fully implementing CODE, a program administrator will directly assign individual roles to those who'll be using the YBR and the MAP. Identifying the primary roles for team members is straightforward. Make people in traditional sales and business development functions the designated Prospectors, responsible for farming and hunting new opportunities. Service or solution providers, such as on-site project managers, field personnel, account managers or program developers, are generally your Technical Experts. Your Closers will come from senior level managers, owners, principles or executive directors. Purchasing agents responsible for finalizing and approving purchases are also Closers. Basically, the Closer role can apply to anyone with the ability and contractual authority to negotiate and close a deal.

One person who embraced the challenge of expanding his role, and whose insights you have seen read, is David Price, the President of Wachter Electric. He initially identified himself as a Technical Expert and Closer, but stepped up to lead Prospecting efforts. In other firms, you might have a hybrid situation where the designated hunters are Business Development people, while everyone else works at farming the core customer base.

When changing culture through CODE, organizations need to ask a question, "What are we trying to achieve?" For some companies, only the business development and sales group will initially adopt this program. However, if the goal is an "all hands on deck" call to action, in which everyone in the organization is required to farm, the administrator should make a stronger effort to differentiate roles and assign responsibilities.

Kourtney Govro, the CEO of Sphere3 Consulting, explains what this looks like:

> "I have a salesperson who is excellent at generating Yellows and can manage the beginning of the Blue phase. But once he gets further into the Blues, he gets excited and nervous and has a hard time pulling them to the Red. He self-implodes at that point, even though he is perfect in the Yellow and early Blue stages. Everybody knows him in our organization and loves him. He can find out all sorts of information.

> "Then I have another sales person who hates the Yellow phase but when she smells blood, she's in and she gets it done. She's gets the P.O.'s. She moves through the organization, gets the questions answered, she's in Red, then she's done.

> "It's interesting to use CODE from a management perspective to really see what people are good at because it helps

you coach them in the areas they are not good at and to align the way you function with them. That's number one.

"Organizationally, our previous structure failed. We had a 40,000-foot view process if you can think of it that way. We just expected people to know how to move into an account or find a lead, kind of do-it-yourself from soup to nuts. Some people couldn't perform from soup to nuts and it would come to a point where it was: sorry, you're out the door because you obviously can't sell. With CODE, we're able to bring the tools to the people on our team and say, 'Yes, we understand that you're a great sales person but we need you to follow a system so we can begin to document and evaluate the way we're interacting with our clients.' Now, after the process implementation, we take a lot of time to train people."

People can fill multiple roles. Take project managers who work onsite and so often hear about new opportunities from other vendors on the same project. Under CODE, their role is primarily Technical Expert (not Prospector). However, in this case, they're also acting as Prospectors farming for opportunities (Yellows). These Technical Experts don't need to sit in on detailed YBR meetings to report their prospecting progress. A weekly phone call is enough for them to hand off the new opportunities to the designated Prospectors who can follow up.

Conclusion: Take Change One Step at a Time

CODE is a flexible framework to adapt to your organization's needs and current status. You might have an ingrained sales culture or a team of technical experts learning to sell for the first time. Regardless, I encourage you to begin in the shallow end. Use your MAP and YBR to focus first on farming your core customer base. Depending on company size, make this the priority for the first six to twelve weeks.

As your team grows more comfortable with the mindset and methodology of CODE, gradually strike out into the deeper end of the pool by hunting for new relationships and opportunities.

Should you represent the firm with a crew of seasoned hunters, keep them readily engaged, but align and integrate them with the CODE principles.

In the next chapter, we will look at implementing CODE to the fullest extent by making the necessary organizational cultural changes to get there, even if that requires an overhaul of the culture itself.

- You need a universal system and common language that clearly defines and communicates where every sales opportunity stands at any given moment.

- CODE provides a color-coded system (YBR) that directly coordinates all of your team's behaviors and interactions with prospects. The team always knows the exact next steps and deadlines associated with each opportunity in order to move the opportunity forward.

- Yellow: These are "golden" opportunities that Prospectors are just uncovering with potential clients. People are exploring a need, the project or opportunity is funded or in the budget, but there's little urgency to meet to discuss it.

- Blue: "Cool down!" These prospects have agreed to meet and discuss details of a specific project, so Technical Experts need to slow down and take the time to fully qualify the opportunity, making sure it's a good match prior to producing a proposal, bid or estimate.

- Red: The opportunity is "red hot", typically has competition if it arrives a red, and requires a Closer to negotiate a deal. (Highest urgency.)

- Green: A yes or no decision has been made and the opportunity was won, lost or killed. Keep track of these post-sales categories to score how well your team manages the sales process. The contacts associated with the project are "evergreen" and rotate back to the MAP.

- When you first create and organize your YBR, consider the systems and organic sales process your organization already has in place. Work with those as you implement CODE and build upon your success.

- Organize your team with clear roles and responsibilities. Everyone who works for your company should know clearly if they are primarily a Prospector, Technical Expert or Closer, and when to fulfill each of those roles. They also need to know if they've been assigned the responsibilities of farming, hunting or both.

- Make change gradually and intentionally by using CODE to farm your core customer base (the first six weeks). When your team has adjusted to the process, use CODE to hunt for new opportunities and customers.

Chapter Seven: Achieve Cultural Change

There are only two certain things about change: It's hard; and most people don't like it.

Clients and friends know me for calling a spade a spade. I realize that implementing change of any kind is challenging. Introducing a system like CODE can and often does *feel messy*. Even for those intuitively applying many of CODE's elements already, formalizing the process can sometimes feel daunting.

How can you dispel some of that apprehension? Anticipate challenges *before* formally engaging in the process. Get your key leaders and policy makers to buy into the change before you try to implement it. Help them understand that the process produces measurable change, but has an organizational learning curve that can be anticipated. Start with where you are and where the company stands (culturally) right now. Employees are being asked to build on existing skills by relating to customers in intentional ways by coordinating the team's efforts through CODE. It's achievable change.

Still, it's *change*. Prepare for potential pushback. Your employees are about to step outside their personal comfort zones and learn to think and operate differently. They may push back, because change can be scary. "What if I try this and fail? What if it doesn't work? Is my job in danger if I can't do this well by next week?" Train your leaders to communicate that the company sees this as an important direction, believes they can reach the new expectations, and is willing to support employees on the learning curve to get there. Recognize that adoption takes time.

When I train companies, I often open by intentionally wearing a nametag that identifies me as "Flavor of the Day," because I know that's exactly how some will view me—as management's latest brainy idea. I know what they're thinking: "Wait long enough, and this too shall pass."

CODE is not a small band-aid for a gaping wound. There's nothing temporary about this "fix." It's a comprehensive response to a major question facing businesses today: How can we get everyone to sell more effectively and consistently—or at minimum, to understand their role in supporting the sales effort? My aim remains the same: to enable organizations to compete in this uncertain economy while bringing relief to employees who must now do more with less. You can only squeeze so much water from a stone, but the environment we're in continuously requires us to find more water, no matter how parched the stone.

In this climate, CODE offers something very individual: a new skill set that not only makes people more effective at doing their current jobs, but also more prepared for future career transition. People need to know how to sell themselves to win new jobs and contracts. Nearly half the U.S. workforce (an estimated 70 million people) will be free agents or contract-based employees by the year 2020. Who among us will be prepared?

Truly sustainable change demands a lot from people. However, the alternative is unpleasant: to stay with the status quo and accept the painful cycle of feast or famine. That cycle burns people out and leads the organization into a culture of apathy. Whether anyone cares to admit or not, no safe status quo exists in sales. Companies are either moving ahead or falling behind.

CODE provides the method, mindset and tools not only to keep moving ahead, but also to progress in a measurable, vastly more predictable way. When the company's sales become more predictable, employees feel more confident and empowered to control the company's destiny—and, their own.

Now, let's implement CODE.

Taking Inventory

The biggest, best-funded, publicly-traded companies can feel as challenged as tiny start-ups. In small companies, the issues are usually easy to identify and comparatively simple to change. In larger companies, the problems can be spread across departments or divisions and involve a much higher degree of logistical and relational complexity. But the challenges have the same roots, regardless of company size.

It's OK to encounter road bumps when you first begin implementing CODE. Expect it! You *will* encounter road bumps, no matter the size of the organization. A few realities to be aware of as you engage:

- The employees' attitudes toward adopting CODE may run all over the map. Some will be more willing to participate than others. Some will question the amount of change the company "needs", or if now is the "right" time to do it.

- Some may resist change because they already feel overwhelmed. (Even if, ironically, the dysfunction of the old sales process contributes directly or indirectly to their overwhelmed feeling!) They're thinking, "Management is once again asking us to do 'one more thing,' and it's one too many." Usually, those refusing to support the new program usually let their attitude surface on the first day you introduce it.

- Your information on relational assets may be stashed throughout the company, with outdated lists of core customers in file cabinets, new sales recorded in a half-adopted CRM system that only partially matches your needs, and employees privately using their own independent "systems" for managing their workflow.

- People with limited computer skills or abilities may be challenged by the adoption of CODE's primary tools, the MAP and YBR.

- People unaccustomed to thinking of themselves as "salespeople" may resist because they "hate" sales. Or, they are technical specialists who don't feel confident thinking of themselves as relational specialists, even with customers already buying their expertise.

While all of these are legitimate issues, anticipating these potential potholes before you shift into drive can be helpful.

Modeling Behaviors

Some managers may struggle with the new responsibilities. After all, they have to model the new system for everyone else, and motivate the rest of the team to do it, too. They are learning to do it themselves while already teaching others. That's not always an easy task. Key influencers should try to anticipate issues with the transition and address them head on. Spearheading change can humble even the most confident leader. Some non-verbal or introspective people in leadership positions might feel uncomfortable with what simultaneously modeling and promoting change requires of them.

Here's the critical piece: if you want your entire team on board, all of your leaders must stay committed to the behaviors, attitudes and skills critical to the CODE process. Otherwise, employees may take the cue and check out.

During training, I can often tell who is open to the program and who is likely to resist it, by body language alone. My challenge? To limit the influence of peer leaders who openly refuse to buy in. They can undermine the efforts of an entire department. This occurred in a large organization I consulted. The manager of a service department opened up our first progress meeting with a list of reasons why he thought adopting the CODE system would not work:

- The economy is toxic.

- The industry has been commoditized.

- If there were a way to do things better or differently, they would have developed it by now: "Look, I've been in the business for 30 years, and I've seen it all."

After listening respectfully, I responded that things could be improved. I also pointed out that peer companies in the same industry (and city!) were already engaged in the process. They, too, started out with similar concerns. Over time, though, measurable results increased their enthusiasm and drove them to change their position. I explained that adopting CODE is a process. As such, try not to expect instant results, but give it time to take root. Relationships, both inside and outside organizations, need to be nourished. This takes time and patience. Healthy relationships are built on trust, and trust takes time to build.

What happened with this concerned department leader? He eventually changed his thinking (and negative attitudes), but not without three months of intense prodding that finally pushed him across the threshold of adoption. In the first session of another training I conducted, a man just sat there with his arms tightly crossed across his big engineering heart. His body language broadcast how much he disliked and disagreed with the training and its purpose. At break time, he "accidentally" threw a Coke can across the room, almost nailing me in the head (seriously!).

Needless to say, after the session was over, he approached me and expressed his intense dislike of the CODE program. How could I have predicted this? He told me all the reasons why he didn't feel he should have to follow the directive.

The outcome was predictable from day one. He was capable of changing and adapting, but deliberately *chose not to*. He had the relationships and communication skills to make it work, but he refused to change the way he thought about his job description. He didn't want to try.

You know what's interesting about his story? Months after I left my consulting post, he reached out to connect with me on LinkedIn. Management had tired of his attitude and underperformance and he needed to fortify his network for new job opportunities. He quietly shared with me that he uses CODE to manage his own contract job opportunity pipeline. In retrospect, he wrote, perhaps he should have "tried harder."

His story illustrates a hard lesson. Employees can adapt with the support of a company paying to improve their skills or they can fund their own learning curve.

The bottom line? They are going to learn. It doesn't have to be hard, but the approach management takes has everything to do with the response they will encounter. Quite often, it will take a while to get the desired traction, but people will get on board—if not for their organization, then for themselves. Personal and organizational change proceeds methodically, step-by-step. Think marathon, not sprint.

Employees look to their leaders for direction. If leaders are not willing to commit to the process, management must quickly intervene and reach a workable resolution. Nothing deflates the momentum of change or a new process faster than unenthusiastic or uninvolved leaders.

Using the MAP: What to Expect in the First Six Months

Farm. Then hunt.

When implementing CODE, most companies focus on farming their core customer base for the first six weeks. Then, they hunt for new customers. Dream prospects or accounts are the ideal places to focus hunting efforts.

You're hunting for new relationships as much as you are hunting for new sales. By using the 1-5 ranking system to prioritize the organization's MAP relationships, you reveal how these current relationships stand in terms of loyalty to the organization.

This is different from ranking customers by the size or frequency of their purchases. You're looking at the quality and untapped potential of the relationship itself, not just the sales it has already generated. From there, you can determine how best to focus your efforts to improve the loyalty of your longstanding customers. Along the way, you can more intentionally develop the budding relational loyalty of the new customers you nurture.

Here's two examples of what this might look like:

- In long-established service divisions (B2B or B2C), huge lists of contacts considered to be 'moving targets' might already exist. When you develop your MAP, the goal is to narrow down and prioritize the top, say, 25 targets. Get the ball rolling with a manageable goal, learn from the experience and gradually target your way through the entire MAP. Establish a reasonable starting place. I will typically ask the leaders of groups or divisions to lead the discussion to identify the top targets so the team can reach consensus on the top choices and also establish ownership over the selection process.

- For divisions handling large national accounts, start by listing core contacts within those accounts. Then name the location of the branch or division within the client company, including the name and title of the contact and whoever manages it internally. Lastly, assign rating numbers for each contact.

Rating people (rather than companies) helps teams identify and prioritize possible loopholes in account penetration, especially when you need internal referrals to effectively farm certain core accounts. Use common sense here: ask people you already know to introduce you to the key people you don't know yet. While this may seem obvious, it'd surprise you the number of companies that do not effectively farm within national accounts.

Use the MAP to agree on key priorities, to effectively target your actions and to monitor and measure progress. If you are using a spreadsheet or your own system, be sure to **label each rating with a date/time stamp**.

It can take some time to adjust to this measuring system, but it can dramatically improve a person's ability to prioritize their efforts to leverage existing relationships and establish new ones. It makes the sales process more human, because management requires employees to build relationships, not just generate transactions.

In fact, you can actually use the MAP to set individual employees' performance goals according to how they manage relationships with customers. For example, set 90-day goals for Prospectors that are based on the ranking system. How many of their target 4's did they convert to 5's? (See Tip #3 in the Tips and Tools for a few suggestions for employees approaching and communicating with customers to farm and hunt for their business.)

Frequently, my clients will build organizational charts of their current key customers to identify missing contact information and rate the targets for personal referrals or introductions. It takes a concentrated effort to effectively inventory and classify key relational assets on the MAP. That's why I suggest starting with just the top 25. It breaks down the elephant-eating task into "doable" bites. Another angle is to assemble an organizational chart for major clients, which can serve as a satisfying starting point, because it will deliver your team immediate value.

Identifying Whites from the MAP and Assigning Primary Responsibilities

After you have started building your MAP, identify and assign individual relational priorities that are lifted from the MAP. Transfer these priorities to the White Lists. Typically, they amount to one to five names per week, per person. Start with focusing on farming core customer accounts. Over time, as your team becomes familiar with the process, you'll shift Prospecting efforts to hunting for new customers.

To start, team leaders should identify MAP targets and, where appropriate, help Prospectors who are acting as hunters with their individual MAP targets. Prospectors should pick relational targets in industries who:

- Correspond to what they are passionate about

- Correspond to their expertise or proficiency

- Make strategic sense for the organization

When a contact is identified as a White but is unknown to anyone in the company—and no one steps forward to "own" the target—the team leader or administrator should select the team member most likely to form a relationship with the target and assign it to them.

Consider the following questions:

- Who in the organization is most naturally qualified to undertake hunting efforts?

- What role should the organization's Technical Experts play in supporting these efforts?

- While understanding the differing levels of buy-in and behavior change, who should attend the MAP and YBR Progress Meetings to report next steps?

The implementation phase of CODE provides your team with a golden opportunity to bring their interests and passions to the table and to choose targets about which they feel excited. One of the most effective ways to encourage success in hunting for new opportunities is to let Prospectors step forward to volunteer. Who do they *want* to work with? Roger Hagen, Sales Manager at GENESYS, gives an example of this dynamic:

> "I can't draw the path [from a White to an opportunity] on the MAP for my guys. They really have to find their own path to get in with that target. That's why it has to start

with them selecting an opportunity they think they can bring value to.

"For example, the Harley-Davidson account was a good match for one of my guys—Jake. He rides motorcycles, especially Harley-Davidsons, so he had connection there. He knows that Harley is one of these companies that people are very passionate about. They have a lot of brand loyalty to Harley-Davidson. Right there, it's an advantage if their supplier has some feeling—some understanding—of the kind of people who like Harley-Davidson. It was a good fit for Jake because he has something instantly in common with the people he's talking to. He saw the natural connection for himself, which was less than obvious just looking at the MAP.

"For individuals, choosing a MAP target means they feel they might be able to get a buy-in. In another meeting, there was a guy assigned to Nestle-Purina who just didn't want to 'eat the dog food,' as the term applied in this case. He didn't feel a connection and we found it was a better fit for someone else at the table.

"[The important thing] for me is that my guys get excited about jobs that they want to work on."

When implementing the CODE system, think of three Blocks of Focus:

| **MAP =**
Who You Know
& Want to
Know | **Weekly Whites =**
Contact Names
to Target | **YBR =**
Pipeline of
Opportunities |

The MAP is about People, Weekly Whites are about Priorities, and the YBR is about Projects.

Once you've assigned roles and responsibilities, everyone in the sales effort should possess:

- Individual lists of Whites selected from the MAP (so they know where to Prospect). This can be one to five names per day or per week depending on their organizational position.

- A clear idea about the opportunities for which they're responsible, and the next steps for engaging them (as indicated on the YBR).

- A clear understanding of how their primary role coordinates with others on the team (so performance expectations are positioned accordingly).

Managing Expectations from the Beginning, to Success and Beyond

Your initial goal in implementing CODE is to manage expectations around the certain changes about to happen. Communicate what you realistically expect team members to do at each stage. Regularly affirm that it will take repetition, time and practice to adapt—and that is okay. It may feel messy at the beginning. That's okay, too!

From time to time, people have asked me, "So, what's the most dangerous part of this process?" It's when a company is running lean (read: profitable) and they've experienced a sustained level of success. It may sound counterintuitive, but when a company passes the pain threshold of adoption, that's when people and attitudes might relax and start to slide. They may become less intentional and urgent with their efforts, resulting in creeping organizational apathy. While they've reached a level of success, the temptation may be to revert to passivity.

Ironic, isn't it? We busily service the new work, and then forget what it takes to generate it in the first place. It's a classic trap.

There are two reasons why organizations have a difficult time aggressively focusing on new business when they've posted strong gains. First, new people and contacts can be harder to identify when we have achieved a level of success and enjoyed the accompanying comfort zone. The more comfortable we are, the less likely we seek new relationships. Why seek dates when you are happily married?

The second reason? It takes team accountability and planning—where everyone is clear about goals and next steps—to give team members the push and confidence to leave their comfort zones for potentially unfamiliar territory. New opportunities lie in that unfamiliar territory.

Here's another question people often ask upfront. "How long does implementing this change take?" Expect a healthy six months. You have to implement CODE and engage in order to change the company mindset. If you've been in business more than ten minutes, you know that sustainable change takes time.

For more details on what to expect, look at the back of this book in the Tips & Tools at Tip # 4: a week-by-week summary of what to expect during the change process.

Conclusion: Agree to Take Off, Lean Back and Trust Your Pilot...

I compare the turbulence during the first six weeks of implementing CODE to taking off in a plane for the first time. Passengers sit down, strap on a seat belt, and trust the pilot to get them safely to their destination. As the plane takes off, *things can feel out of control*. Reaching altitude can also be bumpy. But when the plane reaches its cruising altitude, everything smoothens out and flying becomes comfortable, almost natural. Then the drink cart shows up. It caters to a tendency to get sloppy, because the whole process of flying now feels familiar.

Following implementation, the number one danger in working with the CODE system is that people get overly familiar with the basics and stop working with focus and perseverance.

The process becomes so simple, but it works best with another, more behavioral component: intention. A mindset of intention keeps you focused on what's mission-critical and drives you to your next success.

Think about how you might respond to the creeping weight gain that often follows weight loss: you know what to do, but you don't follow through unless you are held accountable. Don't let the high of initial success distract you from the goal of long-term, sustained and exponential growth.

As the great David Sandler wrote in *You Can't Learn to Ride a Bike at a Seminar*, the only way to learn is through experience. That takes time, commitment, and a true connection to the meaning behind the effort.

People learn by doing.

- Yes, change is hard. People don't tend to like it.

- Manage your implementation of CODE by clearly communicating your expectations to leaders and employees. Identify what is required of them at each stage of the process.

- Communicate the vision: to focus the company on relationships, to improve sales, and to answer the employees' key question: what's in it for me? Give your employees the transferrable skills necessary to survive in a free agent economy.

- Review your organization's specific situation (employees, attitudes, workflows and databases of customer information). Plan your implementation of CODE accordingly.

- For the transition to succeed, emphasize that leaders must model CODE by using it themselves. Get engaged, cross-train and coach people with ideas of how to make prospecting a natural part of their workflow.

- Transition to the MAP and YBR. Articulate specific and measurable goals.

- Identify Whites from the MAP for Prospectors to farm and hunt. If appropriate, encourage Prospectors to choose their targets according to their passions, expertise and the company's broader strategy.

- Don't let success slow down your growth. Beware of organizational apathy.

- People learn by doing.

Chapter Eight: Work the YBR Pipeline

If you can't measure it, you can't improve "it."

The MAP and YBR work together to help sales teams stay in sync. Employees return over and over to these two strategic reference points in the CODE process to record their efforts and determine what to do next. The MAP and YBR offer up-to-date snapshots of an organization's relational network and all the opportunities in play. Like the primary muscles that make up the left and right side of the heart, the MAP and YBR work to circulate new business (oxygen) throughout the organization. Both need regular updating to maintain and enhance your organization's performance throughout the sales process.

Once you implement CODE, there are two types of progress meetings that can serve as a regular part of the work schedule: a weekly review of the YBR and a by-monthly review of MAP Whites (priority people or contacts). Less often—perhaps monthly or quarterly—you need to hold a MAP meeting with leadership to review general progress in broadening the MAP and improving targets' 1-5 ratings. If you engage in lengthy sales cycles, perhaps weekly is too often to have progress meetings, but someone needs to check in on CODE performance measures (Scorecard) and system accountability. Leadership needs to identify what's best in terms of group reporting, perhaps starting weekly and adjusting as they see fit once you're through the implementation process.

The two meetings concerning MAP Whites and the YBR toggle back and forth. They monitor individual and team progress. Knowing that an accountability meeting is on the schedule for Friday keeps employees on task to relate to the customer sooner, rather than later. The MAP White List Meeting identifies top priority prospects or customers. The YBR Meeting improves your team's coordination in managing pipeline-related issues. The information discussed at the YBR meeting identifies next steps, organizational capacity and cross training for coaching moments. It also provides a platform for establishing better communication among operating departments.

When you launch CODE, your company's cultural playing field and rules change. Everyone from every department is on the same team, with the same goal: to cultivate relationships into predictable sales opportunities. To strengthen the culture of trust among your leaders and rank-and-file employees, strive to improve team communication until everyone can say with confidence, "I can speak your language and you can speak mine. We are on the same team. Our goal is to nurture relationships and share information that results in profitable work."

For some companies, this level of teamwork might feel like a much-needed breath of fresh air.

Interpreting the Company YBR

After you apply the standard definitions of Yellows, Blues and Reds by color-coding all existing opportunities, assess the status of the current YBR pipeline. (Reminder: As you are making the conversion to the YBR, slow down and pay attention to avoid mislabeling opportunities.) Once you've labeled the opportunities in progress, take a step back. Look at the YBR as a whole. Trends, breakdowns or shining successes might jump out at you. It might be the first time you've ever seen the state of your sales displayed in such a colorful snapshot.

No matter what problems you might uncover during this early assessment, understand that the analysis provides management with an opportunity to reevaluate the effectiveness of current business development and marketing strategies. The color distribution across the pipeline vividly reveals the strengths or weaknesses of those attending to it. Thoughtful evaluation should produce better questions and strategies on how to coach for skills or address behaviors required to achieve better results.

What's an "ideal" healthy pipeline look like? For every fully qualified Red, you should have twice as many Blues, and six times as many Yellows. To illustrate this idea, you might have 5 Reds, 10 Blues, and 30 Yellows. That's a healthy pipeline:

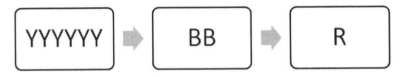

Now let's look at the flip side. What I often see during the early stages of applying CODE are:

- Too many Yellows (people who say they are going to do something, but have no budget or funding)

- Too few Blues (caused by not taking the time to properly qualify opportunities)

- Too few Reds (Blues aren't closing, so there's no urgency to managing the pipeline, as opportunities are not properly qualified)

- Too many Reds (competing purely on price or bidding)

- No tracking of Greens (lost or killed leads drop away, never to be considered again, and not recycled in terms of relationships)

I'd like to take you through each of these problems, one color at a time, followed by solutions I recommend to arrive at the ideal proportion of Yellows, Blues and Reds. Remember, the fundamental goal of CODE is to help you create and maintain a steady and predictable (i.e., healthy) pipeline of sales.

Too Many Yellows

When prospects say they're ready to move forward with a solution, product or service, and funding or a budget exists, label them Yellow. You still don't know the details, and you'll need a face-to-face meeting to learn more, but the lead is solid. It just isn't urgent yet.

What if you drop by to tell someone about the services of your company and the meeting is informational? Does this "meeting" qualify as a Blue? No. If there's no qualified and specific opportunity, it's not a Blue meeting. It's just two people getting together to talk and nurture a relationship.

Now, what if the YBR has a disproportionately high number of Yellows? It may suggest the sales team isn't properly qualifying the prospects by making sure that a "real" opportunity has been uncovered. They may be mislabeling their efforts to nurture the relationship, but not moving forward because they really haven't identified someone with both need and intention (read, *budget*) to buy. There can be a tendency to leave Yellows on the back burner. Maybe the sales team isn't clear about how to define a "good prospect." They might be tracking opportunities that should be categorized as "nice relationships," likely to go no further.

A further challenge in managing Yellows is the potential for aging callback dates. Too often, organizations let opportunities go dormant because no one takes the initiative to follow up on a scheduled basis. What happens? The next time the opportunity pops up on the team radar, it's already "on the streets." In other words, it's a Red opportunity about to close, and now there's stiff competition to your company. This severely limits the team's ability to engage in relationship development and positioning strategies.

Not Enough Blues

Let's say you confirm a meeting with a prospect to qualify the scope of a funded need or opportunity. You might even classify the meeting as an estimating or budgeting session. In doing so, this lead becomes a Blue.

I call a pipeline with too few Blues "The Blue Hole." There may be a healthy number of Yellows and Reds, but too few Blues relative to them. This is typical for many companies with which I've worked. It usually indicates organizational self-sabotage, like rushing through the qualification process or rushing to Red.

There's one exception. In companies that take inbound service calls, the contact would be classified as a Yellow, but it might switch directly to Red if you provide an estimate for services during the course of the call. In the Business-to-Consumer world, the sales process condenses rapidly. But even then, when discussing price, there's a certain psychology behind managing the conversation from Yellow to Red. Blue qualification questions may still apply.

The idea of managing opportunities in a thorough, scaled manner—going from Yellow to Blue to Red—is really a mindset. Everyone on your team should adopt this way of thinking. When responding to a request for service, slow down, listen, and focus on ways to manage the prospect's expectations.

Too Few Blues: Moving Too Fast

Many organizations have a tendency to operate in one of two modes:

- Scrambling to find leads (generating yellows), or

- Cranking out mounds of proposals or bids (reds) and hoping something eventually sticks

Either way, they don't have a method for intentionally slowing down the process to improve their rate of return. Make sure the lead is a good fit before investing time and money to evaluate the scope of the project and adequately develop the bid, proposal or estimate.

When dealing with Blues, one of your primary tasks is to continue developing a rapport with the customer. Build trust, and feed their level of appreciation for possible solutions your organization can provide. Focus on managing expectations on both sides and establishing a mutual understanding of value as it relates to price. Do this while positioning and differentiating the solutions offered.

For example, let's say you're creating promotional tools for a prospect. You might have a menu of 20 items that have worked for other clients. But you need to whittle it down to the eight to ten items *they* need. When you work this out with the prospect, you build communication, trust and appreciation. You're that much closer to bidding and taking the prospect to Red.

When the sales process involves multiple prospect meetings, enter each meeting with a clear agenda and purpose while steadily moving toward a close. (If, at any time, an agenda is not clear, or a prospect seems hesitant about the meeting's purpose, a Blue can revert to Yellow.)

Few Reds

Once you fully qualify a prospect and they request a proposal (estimate, bid or RFQ/RFP), the Blue opportunity converts to a Red.

What if an organization discovers too few Reds in the YBR relative to the number of Blues? Often, there's a breakdown in the system to qualify solid opportunities. Equally problematic is using price alone to establish Reds over Blues. Too much emphasis on price favors quantity over quality in the pipeline. Having too many Reds reflects the very dynamic CODE works to counter: commoditization, or competing on price instead of value.

Once you've submitted a proposal or estimate, a Closer confirms its receipt. This is exceedingly important. It's not enough to depend on technology such as email, faxes or messages. The Closer needs to:

- Place a confirmation call or email to a specific person who is "in the know."

- Explicitly request a response or confirmation of the call or email.

Clients have transferred millions of dollars in projects to less qualified companies because of simple email or faxing snafus involving their first choice.

Too Many Reds Lost

How many lost Red leads is too many? I cannot overemphasize the importance of this question. Within it lies your short- and long-term future as a growing company.

The answer will depend on the industry, your sales team's experience, and the organization's overall pricing strategy, plus many other factors. The most common reasons, though, are that sales teams:

- Move too fast and do not fully qualify the opportunity.

- Fail to establish rapport or a relationship with the decision-maker.

- Fail to establish a clear understanding of value verses price that allows both parties to determine whether the opportunity is a good fit for both sides.

- Do not fully prepare for negotiating and closing the deal.

- Do not designate a Closer with the proper authority or ability to negotiate and close the deal.

However, if you work in a focused, intentional way with prospects, especially in the first two phases of the sales process, you'll enjoy far greater predictability and success.

Managing the YBR: Prioritizing Time for Progress Meetings

Reds

I recommend that teams start the meeting by focusing on Red opportunities. Do so in order of descending revenue value and anticipated close dates. Depending on the number of Red opportunities in the pipeline, be strategic about how you allocate organizational time and manpower resources. This is very important.

While kicking off the CODE process, you usually won't be able to cover every item on the YBR. Focus on either the most pressing opportunities or those offering the most potential revenue. Or both. Confirm who is serving as the Closer and establish clear closing strategies.

Blues

Most prospects ask for two things: free consulting and price. You might be eager to provide free consulting in an attempt to win a prospect's favor and business. Slow down! Qualify the Blue. If you ask for and exchange critical information, you'll ultimately create mutual respect. This is important to set conditions for disclosure, as each party needs to clearly state their definition of price relative to value. Should you and the prospect fail to see eye-to-eye at this level, you probably won't be a good fit, no matter how much "free consulting" you provide. Better to face the bad news now than in the Red phase—or worse, after a contract has been awarded.

A client of mine made a valuable point to members of his team. "Every month," he said, "the company offers each of you a bucket of money" (the cost of time and internal resources to convert prospects to customers). "If this money is spent on unqualified leads, it can add up to considerable overhead costs to the company." He concluded, "Slow down and be selective. Use eight questions to qualify your Blue opportunities before committing money from your bucket."

The idea of slowing down may not feel or seem practical. We live in an accelerated world where today's excited conversation about a new opportunity can become tomorrow's sad lament of what-ifs. However, the great ones in business, just like the great sports stars, know that when impulse suggests accelerating, there's nothing better than to slow down. While your competitors race for a quick-hit solution, invest time to craft a *lasting* solution. Your reputation depends on it. So do your referrals.

> *"I first learned this idea through CODE training," said Roger Hagen of GENESYS. "Customers seek as much free consulting as they can get and then invariably ask for the lowest price to go with it. An approach we now use to combat this dynamic is transparency: 'We are here offering free consulting. We're going to share our opinion and you're getting this **one** plant visit for free.'*

> *"By working in such an honest, direct manner with the customer, we can establish what needs to be done, even while defending the value we're providing. At the end, it's a take-it-or-leave-it kind of thing. If the customer doesn't respond well to this approach, then it's probably not a good fit anyway."*

Can you see how mindset impacts the issue of defending value in dealing with the customer? This holds true for all types of businesses. If you get stuck in the free consultation/low price dynamic, you will trap your company into low-paying, labor-intensive projects that greatly diminish your potential to win the high-end business you deserve.

Yellows

When you assess Yellow opportunities, determine the quantity and quality of information associated with each. Ask yourself:

- Is there a callback date?

- Who is following up on the lead?

- Is the Prospector engaged with the right people to obtain current or inside knowledge?

- Has the Prospector pulled together industry, political or personal contacts to gather or confirm more information about the opportunity?

- What needs to happen next to convert the lead to Blue?

- Are we effectively monitoring progress?

Qualifying Prospects

Managing opportunities is important throughout the sales process, but thoroughly managing Blues takes special attention.

There are Eight Questions for qualifying Blues. First determine where prospects stand on the experience curve. Have they previously bought solutions from similar organizations? Are they first-time purchasers? Even if they've bought before, find out about their previous experiences. Chances are, something has disappointed them, or they would not be "shopping around."

"Inexperienced" Prospects

You will deal with many prospects buying products or services for the first time. This is how new relationships start and business grows. These prospects have no frame of reference for potential issues to address for the process to move forward smoothly. They have no idea what can hurt them. They're typically unaware of the complexity of issues that may arise. They also have a limited sense about the level of detail and effort required for a comprehensive estimate. Finally, when it comes to determining the pricing of a project, they may be naïve.

Inexperienced prospects sometimes look at dealing with vendors as a "price" or negotiation game. Others perceive all vendors to be the "same"—one as good as the other. Those prospects will request proposals to position one firm against another in terms of price. That's a big mistake.

When you deal with inexperienced prospects, slow them down. Use your experience, knowledge and position to address the "myths" they may harbor. The top five myths:

- All providers are the same

- Everything comes down to price

- Everything is negotiable

- I can take all the time I need to do this

- I have needs that are completely unique

Sound familiar? I've encountered these myths so many times that I considered printing them on t-shirts and handing them out at trade shows.

The "Experienced" Prospect

Virtually all salespeople, especially Closers, would rather deal with experienced prospects. They have purchased products or services before, and their attitudes often reflect their previous experiences. "Something" has likely happened with their current or previous solution provider, or they wouldn't be talking to you. They understand the value of good service far better than inexperienced prospects, but that comes with a caveat: their expectations. Managing their expectations presents you with three particular communication challenges:

- **Face Time = Trust:** Assuming the prospects have encountered some type of negative experience, foster trust so they will reveal the details of what happened.

- **Probe for Pain:** Find out what they are trying to overcome or change by working with someone new.

- **Define Success:** Ask the prospects to disclose upfront what they expect from the transaction (what's their definition of success?). This enables the Prospector to effectively manage or even change expectations about price, solution (proprietary disclosure) and competition.

The Eight Questions for Qualifying a Blue Opportunity

Your primary goal throughout the qualification process is to establish rapport with prospects while you assess their position on the assumptions curve. Depending on the size of the job and how many meetings it requires, you may casually weave the eight questions among a few detailed conversations, or you might discuss them over several structured meetings. Whatever the case, don't treat these questions as a simple checklist.

A Technical Expert (or whoever is qualifying the Blue) should have the freedom to determine where and when to ask these eight questions. *Eventually ask every question.* Assumptions kill deals, and they need to be avoided at all costs when qualifying an opportunity.

Question 1: Is there a timeline for the project? And, is there financing or a budget in place?

Are prospects seriously considering making a purchase? Or are they just fishing for information (or free consulting)? Ask about timeline, budget and financing and you'll know the answer. To the extent they indicate a firm date for making a decision and a real budget or financing, you'll know their level of motivation to move forward.

If there's a timeline but no budget for a project or purchase, then prospects are *not* ready to move forward, regardless of what they might say. Think of someone seeking to buy a home, but that person has not yet consulted a mortgage office or a bank. Until they do, they cannot be considered a truly qualified buyer. When the answer is 'yes' to this question, you've got a confirmed yellow.

Question 2: Who is the decision-maker?

Is the prospect the decision-maker? If not, have you as the Prospector identified one? Until then, you can only proceed on assumptions. At some point, you have to confirm the viability of the opportunity with a decision-maker. If a group makes decisions, such as a committee or board of directors, ask this question: Is there a structured process to make a decision?

Your goal is to meet with as many group members as possible to establish what is most important to the majority. You want to understand and reveal as many factors as possible, all of which may affect the outcome of a purchasing decision.

Question 3: What specific criteria will the prospect use to select a vendor or review the proposal?

Many decision-makers pay lip service to the statement, "We value quality over price." You might have to work a little harder to unearth their actual determining factors. The more time a Prospector or Technical Expert spends with a prospect, the more they will discover about what the prospect values most.

Typically, prospects resort to three major factors to determine if a proposed solution will meet their needs:

- A timeframe for solution delivery. Can a company move fast enough to meet their needs?

- Additional value. Has the provider thought through the scope of the project? Does it provide a "value add solution"?

- Access to the provider's "A" team.

Find out the determining criteria for selecting a provider or awarding a contract. You should be able to validate the prospect's needs and show whether your organization can meet their requirements.

Question 4: Who is the competition?

A client of mine met with a prospect about an opportunity, unaware of an existing competitor with whom the prospect had a long history. They were, in fact, good friends. After many meetings, my client was all but convinced he'd closed the deal. At the last minute, without consulting my client, the prospect called his old friend to shop the numbers. My client lost a multi-million dollar contract over a very negotiable $90,000.

Afterward, it became quite evident to my client and I that the prospect went through the motions of obtaining another set of numbers to satisfy his company's guidelines. Most likely, he never had any intention of awarding the contract to my client. While these situations are not entirely avoidable, do ask straightforward questions about previous experiences with other providers and the role competition may play in going forward. You don't need to spend time working for business that will not happen. That is time taken away from prospects that really will want to work with you.

Now for the positive: My client turned the loss into an opportunity. He wrote a clear case study describing how the company had lost a deal over a relatively small sum. He used the study in meetings with future prospects to prompt frank (and early) discussions on the importance of disclosure.

The bottom line: *ask about the competition.*

Question 5: Has the proprietary nature of the organization's proposed solution been addressed?

As mentioned earlier, I advise my clients that prospects are looking for two things: price and free consulting. I recommend they make a conscious effort to defend their expertise and knowledge.

Ryan Neighbors, the Vice President of NCCI, described how as general contractors, they often accepted that they had to give away their best technical ideas and innovations in order to land projects. Then they observed as prospects shopped their proposals and ideas to cheaper bidders. NCCI's customers had routinely asked the company to draw up value-engineered schematics for prospective projects, but then ultimately delivered the blueprints to the lowest-bidding contractor. His company lost thousands of dollars in potential revenue by not having tools in place to defend their value. Clients exploited the value of their resources and approach. How maddening!

"After going through CODE, we realized we had been giving away our most valuable product–our expertise–for free," Neighbors said. "We now require customers to sign a confidentiality agreement or at least acknowledge our proprietary approach and value engineering before providing our solutions. Not only does this save us from working for our competitors for free, it also underscores our position as experts in our field."

As I mentioned before, "free consulting" falls into a tricky category. A Technical Expert might spend a significant amount of time educating an inexperienced buyer, estimating a proposal or scoping a project. This could either be wasted time, or a solid relationship-building strategy, a positive investment of the organization's time that may provide a long-term return.

While providing expertise, opinions or knowledge, Prospectors should always be intent on gathering information from prospects to move the opportunity forward in the YBR. However, if it appears the prospects do not respect the proprietary nature of the solution, it is probably not a good fit. Move on!

Question 6: How do Prospects define value? What are their assumptions about price?

This question of price versus value is significant. Does the prospect appropriately value the solution the organization is prepared to deliver? What a prospect initially requests, and what an organization ultimately delivers, can be two very different things. Roger Hagen of GENESYS Systems spells this out:

"We try hard to get our customers to define the important issues, like their scope and their schedule, what they want done and when they want it done," he says. "We tell them

that the cost is the dependent variable—that after putting all that in the hopper, the price is what falls out. In fact, we use the term 'cost' instead of 'price' whenever we're discussing it with them because **the cost is a function of what they want to buy.**

"Since we represent many different product lines, we're really not competing on a cost per item, per pound of steel, how many options are included, or whatever. With our customers, it's a question of, 'How much labor are we going to put into this to get your return on investment? Where is the point where we're going to maximize that return?' That way, we haven't spent so much money to overbuild the customer a solution. This whole approach aligns with CODE's logic of price versus value."

GENESYS salespeople do not begin with a prospect's budget and work backwards. They first understand what the prospect seeks, *establish common definitions of value*, and only then arrive at a price. GENESYS is prepared to deliver a fixed unit of value. The more value the prospect requests, the higher the final price. If the prospect wants a lower price, they must be prepared to receive lesser value.

Even in a commodity industry, not everything is equal. Two companies can supply the same apples, but if one company has better customer service, on-time deliveries, a more responsive accounting department, and a more pleasant attitude, the Prospect will not compare "apples to apples." They will jump to the company with better service.

During the lead qualification phase, Prospectors should seek to differentiate their organization as much as possible from the competition. Clearly define the value the organization will deliver, to prevent easy comparison with other providers. Emphasize uniqueness. Most prospects want a clear numeric value assigned to their problem, desires or goals. It is your responsibility to discover the deeper issues around expectations—and their related value—and then craft a solution that specifically addresses those expectations.

Question 7: What is the decision-making process?

Several times, I've witnessed companies try to make sales when they've failed to come to a clear agreement on the qualifying questions. Consequently, the Closers were given the runaround, sometimes for months, while the prospects delayed in making a decision. Some delays are unavoidable. But if a prospect commits to a date, Prospectors should hold them accountable. If they won't honor that commitment, it's a warning light that they won't honor others, either.

It's okay not to find the 'right fit' with a Prospect. It's much better to identify the key issues ahead of time. You don't want to invest immense amounts of employee time in doomed opportunities. Avoid last-minute losses by qualifying the prospect, especially by establishing a clear understanding of their decision-making process.

Question 8: What are our next steps to move the opportunity through the pipeline?

Your sales team should ask this question after every interaction with prospects. It applies to every point in managing the YBR, though it is especially important in evaluating Blues. If, after fully qualifying an opportunity, the Prospector or Technical Expert determines it's not viable, the organization may want to take a pass.

Many sales teams never stop to consider turning down a sale, but it is just as important to take unviable opportunities out of the pipeline as it is to keep moving forward with truly strong opportunities. The prospect's respect and goodwill toward the provider is more important than winning any opportunity. A mismatch between what your organization can provide and what prospects expect can lead to long-term problems. It can undermine your credibility and reputation, and the prospects' confidence in engaging your organization for any future work.

Conclusion

The importance of asking solid questions that build rapport and respect cannot be understated. In the prospect's mind, you should be the expert that guides the use of their most valuable asset: time. Be the kind of person who graciously arrives well prepared for each meeting. Be perceived as the company readily sharing solutions, but smart enough to protect and establish the value of the solutions you propose.

Most importantly, be the honest soul that tells them from day one that this process requires trust and disclosure, so you can identify solutions to meet their needs. Provide for them what they want for themselves. It's up to you to establish that level of trust and respect to draw out of them what they want, over the course of several meetings. Then it's a win/win.

When you hit a wall and sense a prospect is not affording you the respect of disclosing the information you need to meet their needs, remember one thing: *you've got the power.* Determine where they fall in your organization's internal priorities, and consider the time you plan to invest responding to their request for a proposal. Handling Blues is all about time invested to build rapport, trust and disclosure. If done well, it's time well spent for both parties.

- Hold two types of progress meetings appropriate to your sales cycle: 1) A MAP Whites meeting to assign new targets to Prospectors and check in on progress; and 2) A YBR meeting to review the status and next steps associated with all opportunities in the pipeline.

- Keep a healthy YBR pipeline with 6 Yellows to every 2 Blues, and 6 Yellows and to every 1 Red.

- Address the symptoms underlying the problem if you have: too many Yellows, too few Blues, too few Reds, too many Reds lost, or no tracking of Greens whatsoever.

- Prioritize your time with Reds, Blues and Yellows and learn to deal effectively with both inexperienced and experienced prospects.

- Communicate clearly the value of your solution. Don't get trapped in the cycle of free consulting or low-paying jobs.

- Use the Eight Questions to qualify prospects. Invest your time and resources in deals that are the best fit for your company.

- Coach the people you have engaging with the YBR in behavioral improvement. Identify areas of questionable team performance in your pipeline and privately coach individuals for better performance.

Chapter Nine: Progress Meetings and Driving Accountability

CODE will perform exactly to the degree you implement it. A big part of that concerns available time. Time must be managed wisely. Every employee's work hours (and yours) must count. In today's economic reality, they must also directly or indirectly contribute to the sales process. Is your company focused on the call for "all hands on deck"? How efficiently are you using time to better develop customer relationships?

The MAP provides immeasurable value to how you organize your relational inventory. Once you've drafted the MAP and converted your sales pipeline to the YBR, anyone engaged in hunting and farming will be responsible for updating his or her progress on both tools. The review process then shifts between two types of progress meetings: the MAP Whites and the YBR.

MAP Whites Meeting Overview

If you are manually running the process, I recommend you hold MAP White meetings at least twice a month for Prospectors. They can review the team's progress against targets lifted from the MAP and transferred to the White Lists. If you are running the process on a CRM or other technology, you may have a more streamlined process of name distribution. Or, you may be utilizing the power of 1BLACKBOOK™ to automate distribution of Whites across the enterprise so you can automate the need for individual or unit progress on this front.

The overall purpose of this meeting is to review and update progress on the MAP while determining next steps for individual Whites (potential prospects). To keep the group focused, ask the following questions:

- Did you make an effort to call, email or connect with a new contact? If so, was it a quality interaction? Or was it a cursory attempt? Is our rating on the contact accurate?

- What's the current quality (state) of the relationship based on past interactions? (+ or -)

- Are the next steps clear for improving the relationship or nurturing the prospect? How is our past performance on other projects or jobs we've completed? Are they satisfied with our work?

- Did you ask the prospect to give you referrals or let you know about upcoming opportunities? Are there new initiatives underway with their company?

- When was the last contact made with a potential prospect?

MAP White meetings keep the team up to speed about what's happening with core customers. After a certain period of time, depending on the organization, the emphasis will shift to updating hunting efforts. By then, your team members will have made a deliberate effort to confirm the loyalty of your core customers.

What happens when Whites do not respond after three or more attempts at contact? Or you have deemed them unsuitable for the organization? Relay a message that all further efforts will cease if they don't respond, but be sensitive to their preferred channel of communication. Social media provides an excellent opportunity to maintain a personal relationship even if the professional relationship is lagging. If they have any interest at all, they will respond. If not, remove the contact from the White List and select another (or others) from the MAP for subsequent meetings. Keep all MAP updates in a centralized database or spreadsheet, accessible to all meeting participants.

Don't pursue a MAP White target blindly. Prospectors should determine if there's an established relational route. Who has already cleared the road? Is there a person inside the target company (or elsewhere) who can give you a key introduction, or some insight? Is there anyone in your organization with a relationship with someone connected to the target company?

When was the last time you asked this question of *all* your employees? You might be surprised, shocked and delighted to learn that someone of little influence at your organization has a brother-in-law running the show at your dream prospects company. I've found from experience this happens more often than not.

YBR Meetings

Hold YBR meetings to review and evaluate the progress of opportunities documented on the YBR spreadsheet. Identify exact next steps to keep opportunities moving through the pipeline toward closing (or removing them if they're unviable). Depending on your organization's sales cycle or industry, plan on a minimum of bi-monthly or monthly meetings. For those with shorter cycles, a weekly meeting or even a daily review may be more appropriate.

YBR meetings have a similar purpose to MAP White meetings: progress reporting. However, the focus in the YBR meeting is to review all active opportunities in the pipeline. To prepare:

- Classify all opportunities and projects as Yellow, Blue or Red. Individual team members need to update or add opportunities to the YBR in a centralized database or spreadsheet if not doing it through 1BLACKBOOK™. Do this *before* the group meeting.

- Call-back dates and notes pertinent to the project should be current and recorded on the spreadsheet. If not, update prior to the meeting, but *don't encourage updates at the meeting.* Otherwise, you will spend the entire meeting focusing on past tasks rather than identifying *what needs to be done.* There's a big difference.

- Your team should list the next steps, update them, and be ready to discuss them.

Make your meetings progressive and forward thinking. Focus on your next steps, based on current YBR data. Discuss the plans for moving forward, rather than reviewing what happened during the past week. There are exceptions, of course. For example, reviewing sales experiences can provide cross-training opportunities for the group.

What is a good litmus test for judging your team's success at recording updates on the YBR? Everyone familiar with the YBR should be able to look at it and immediately understand the next steps required, even if an individual opportunity is not theirs. That way, if the person managing the contact happens to be hit by a bus (God forbid), the next steps should be clear enough for a sixth grader to understand. This ensures an easy transfer to another team member, with minimal disruption to the pipeline.

This is how David Price of Wachter Electric handles this particular meeting:

> *"I monitor sales on a weekly basis in a meeting every Monday morning where my team goes through the entire YBR. Yellows—what's new? Blues—where are we? Reds—how are we going to close these deals?*

> *"I have each of my sales people plan their week ahead on their Outlook calendar and show me what they'll be doing that week. At the end of the week, I ask them to update the YBR with the results. I don't tell them exactly who to call and I don't tell them what to do, but I hold them accounta-*

ble to make sure that they have planned out the week so that they are not just driving around aimlessly."

Establishing Expectations for Progress Meetings

Structure your meetings. Use an agenda to drive efficiency and maximize time. (You can find a sample YBR progress meeting agenda in the Tips & Tools section at the back of this book.) Communicate fully so you can manage individual expectations of your team members, even at the risk of over-communicating. No one likes to arrive at a meeting unprepared (especially Technical Experts, who dislike being perceived as 'wrong'). Leaders need to clearly communicate how to prepare for each type of meeting.

Let me be explicit. From day one, it should be clear *who* needs to attend a meeting, the time frame, the agenda, and how people need to *prepare in advance.* I recommend a one-hour time allowance for each division in the meeting initially, knowing this will reduce significantly (typically to 30 minutes) as people become familiar with the process.

The most important attendees are the company leaders! I'll repeat what I've stated before: team leaders must commit to attending progress meetings and following through on the CODE commitment themselves. When you skip meetings to take calls, attend without involving yourself, or spend the meeting distracted by your electronic devices, *your employees get the message that you are not invested in the meeting.* You'll find yourself back to business as usual: feast or famine, employee disenfranchisement, a lack of cohesion among people or teams, no means for accountability, stagnant sales growth, or all of the above.

Starting on Time

In an hour-long meeting, I recommend 20 minutes dedicated to Reds, 20 to Blues, 10 to Yellows, and 10 for any related topics. For service organizations whose inbound requests go immediately to Red, the breakdown may shift to 30 minutes for Reds, 15 for Blues and 10 for Yellows. Keep the division of time flexible to the needs of your organization. Normally by weeks 12 to 16 of the CODE process, the meetings will condense as team members become more efficient and know what to expect (those one-hour meetings might drop to 30 or 45 minutes).

Staying on Schedule

When I hold progress meetings with clients, I take off my watch and set it in the middle of the table. It's a reminder for all of us to respect the allotted time and to focus. Here is an illustration of why I practice this. During one meeting, I observed a team spend 35 minutes talking about a single $8.5-million job, while ignoring a cluster of $1 million to $2 million jobs. Those bypassed projects added up to $22 million! Leaders need to stay focused on both the forest and the trees. Keep an eye on the Big Picture in order to optimize discussion time on the most viable opportunities in the pipeline.

Guidelines for Discussing Reds, Blues and Yellows

Reds

Start progress meetings with a review of Reds. Go in order of revenue (greatest to least) or anticipated close date. These opportunities are fast moving. The prospect is preparing to make a decision and in a position to deliver revenue to your organization. Basil Hall, VP of Stansell Electric, describes his team's approach to Reds:

"Once an opportunity becomes a Red, we bring in everyone involved—our technical people, division leaders, sales people—and say, 'Okay, this thing is out for bid or proposal. We have a limited amount of time before they make a decision. Do we have any relationships within this company that we can bring to bear? Someone's buddy who will vouch for us? What's our strategy? What are we going to deliver? How do we demonstrate they'll get more value out of our solution? Who's going to carry the ball to the end zone? Who's responsible for what?'

"After we have our plan, we'll get on the phone with the customer before the final pitch to let them know, 'Hey, this is what we will deliver for you.'

"Elizabeth taught us [to pre-close] and it has been invaluable because sometimes you'll discover that the way you've put the package together won't work for them. The guy on the inside might say, 'I'm going to tell you, with the guy running the meeting tomorrow, if you tell him you've done it a little differently, he's going to throw it in the trash. He's not even going to look at it.' And we say, 'Oh, wow—thanks for letting us know.'

"On the other hand, a buddy on the inside might call us up and say, 'I just found out my boss is really interested in this. Do you think you could add it to your presentation next week?'

"By the time you're in the presentation, you should have built the relationship and communicated well beforehand. When they receive your proposal, it should never be a surprise."

This is an excellent example of how to manage relationships for Red opportunities. There should be no surprises. If you have invested enough time to effectively qualify each opportunity, there's usually not much to discuss at the closing. That makes the sales pitch a formality—every organization's dream.

Blues

When you discuss Blues during your YBR meeting, zero in on progress made in answering the Eight Qualifying Questions. Also focus on addressing next agenda items for meetings with the prospect. Drive every interaction with a clear agenda. Review its components at your weekly YBR meetings. Doug Lenny of GENESYS Systems Integrators provides a strong example of why this matters:

"If I'm meeting with an engineer or a customer for a project on Thursday, I say, 'Hey, I'm going to be in the plant on Thursday and I'd like to cover these topics and these items.' That way when I walk in, we're immediately having a conversation. There's no question of, 'Okay, what did you come down here for?' We are constantly working forward together. And if we document and recap every meeting in a follow up email, there's a sense of real progress. At no time do you want any he-said-she-said issues or confusion about what is on the agenda."

Yellows

The last item on the agenda is Yellows. When you team reviews Yellows, keep your discussion centered on lead details as currently understood. Also, determine whether or not callback date(s) have been set. Other guidelines:

- What detailed information has been gathered on this opportunity?

- Who is the contact? A decision maker? Has a relationship been established—and to what degree?

- Is the opportunity budget phase, or funded? How likely is the prospect to commit financial resources to the project or purchase?

- What is the level of urgency?

- What events need to happen for the prospect in order to convert the opportunity to Blue? (What will provide urgency to the situation?)

Stay on top of Yellows and attend to callback dates. Yellows may seem like a low priority, but they are the future gold of your company. Don't sit back and passively wait for the prospect to call. Be proactive.

(For more information, see Implementation Tip #5: A Ten Point Checklist for Reviewing the Health of YBR Progress Meetings.)

A Few Reminders

Give people time to adjust and succeed during the initial application of CODE. Don't overreact if the transition for some is bumpy, but always be mindful of the details. Take small steps forward toward achieving sustainable progress. That's what matters.

CODE tools are intuitive. Take the time to learn to work with them effectively and efficiently. As your team evolves with CODE, keep your eye on the Big Picture as much as the details. Your company is driving the demand for its products by motivating everyone to sell effectively within their roles, and by managing customer relationships in a coordinated, intentional way.

"With CODE, we started getting people who had been here awhile, stakeholders in the company, people in positions of authority, people who had built relationships over the years, and even an owner to sit in a room every week to talk together about the opportunities we were going after," Basil Hall of Stansell Electric recalled. *"Once we started talking about each one, people started saying things like, 'Oh, you know, I went to school with him,' or, 'Hey, I have eight contacts in my address book at that company,' or, 'I've known a guy over there for 20 years. I'll give him a call.' Opportunity by opportunity, we got everyone thinking together, 'How can we win this?' which made all the difference.'"*

What steps do we need to take to win this? Most sales, marketing or customer management systems focus on only one piece of the puzzle. CODE organizes your team to act intentionally with a systematic focus on *both* relationship management and winning sales. "It's important to go over relationships and opportunities as a team," Hall points out. "There was one time before we started doing the CODE meetings that I overheard a salesman in another division say, 'Wow, this is one we really need to win.' I asked who it was. He told me it was with [this company that] he'd been trying to get in for months but couldn't make any headway. 'We're just not in a favorable position and we're getting pushed out.' he said. I told him that my brother-in-law was a decision-maker there and that maybe I could help him.

"The truth is that, yes, it takes a lot of time to get everyone in a room together [to go over the MAP], but you find that what you're trying to do—whether contacting a person or getting an idea on an opportunity—isn't that hard."

Moving from a Transactional Relationship to a Preferred Partnership

Leverage strategic partnerships directly. Meet with your company's strategic partners and key vendors to ask for help. If you draw from MAP targets that may be crossover relationships, you will find it relatively easy to recognize synergies and cross-introduction opportunities for designated people inside targeted companies. Once you identify those people, define specific next steps, joint efforts, and action dates.

Keep in mind that your effort is not just about making partnerships. It's about building the social currency (or trust) necessary for the partnership to succeed and turn a profit.

McKinsey & Co. published a study indicating that half of all business partnerships fail. They generate no revenue beyond the capital invested in the partnership in the first place. Why? *The Harvard Business Review* describes a dynamic where these otherwise smart, successful companies think that the bedrock of their partnership is their contract. They think of the alliance as logistical, not relational. Guess what? Logistics change. All the time.[17]

---

[17] Kaplan, Robert S., David P. Norton, and Bjarne Rugelsjoen. "Managing Alliances with the Balanced Scorecard." *Harvard Business Review*. Jan. 2010. Web. 1 Oct. 2014.

According to *HBR*, these companies focus on the details of the contract, the service level agreement. They tell their middle managers to perform the tasks associated with the partnership. They fail to build the relational alliances necessary to keep the contractual partnership up-to-date and dynamic. It starts out exciting, but then becomes outdated because there isn't enough social currency to keep it current. Outdated becomes burdensome, and burdensome translates rapidly to unprofitable. By the time the companies realize they are losing money, some have given up so much ground that they have fallen behind where they started in the first place, making the entire alliance unprofitable over its lifetime.

HBR recommends that you avoid this dynamic by "moving from a transactional relationship to a preferred partnership." In other words, put relationships first. Let relationships, not transactions, drive the partnership at all levels of the organization. Not just the C-Suite.

How does this impact your sales strategy? It means you have to lay the relational foundation for every layer of the partnership before using the relationship as a highway for transactions.

To move toward a profitable strategic partnership, identify the (potential) partner on your map. You can do the same with industries or new markets, even where you don't yet have any relationships.

Of course, you will have a better chance with anyone you are targeting if you can gain a warm and detailed introduction from a third party (who might explain why there are possible synergies worth exploring).

For target contacts, companies or industries without a clear relational path, the entire team can discuss strategies for establishing contacts. Would a lunch-and-learn be effective? A tour of the company's facilities? Or a meet-and-greet? Don't be afraid to move outside your comfort zone and think creatively about how to connect with strategic targets by teaming up with those who share mutual market interests.

Final Notes on MAP Meetings: Accountability and Coaching

I look for two things above all others when observe MAP meetings: sincere effort and clear progress.

Changes to relational rankings indicate measurable progress (i.e., taking a 1 to a 2, a 2 to a 3, etc.) These aid in dividing farming and hunting activities. For instance, 4's and 3's are the high-priority contacts to nourish, cross-sell, up-sell, request referrals and maintain traction with in core customer accounts. Farm them. The 1's and 2's are targets for hunting efforts. Be sure to define weekly goals for individual team members, such as contacting at least three to five new Whites per week.

A Note to Managers:

During the first six weeks after launching the CODE program, focus on intense farming. Start with the organization's top 25 core customers. Once people have practiced their skills and you've established good traction through farming, the team can expand its hunting efforts. If your organization has a dedicated sales staff, have them focus on hunting from the beginning, since it has already been a part of their job description.

When attending networking events, prepare in advance. Who is attending? Who do you want to meet? If possible, know their faces in advance as well as their names and roles so you can recognize them in a crowded room. Use your time effectively.

A Note to Leaders:

Help people feel more confident about leaving their comfort zones. At events, partner the more outgoing team members with those who need help engaging. Give them a wing man! Utilize experienced salespeople who can model effective conversational approaches to engaging with others. (A great book on this subject is *Never Eat Alone: And Other Secrets to Success, One Relationship at a Time*, by Keith Ferrazzi and Tahi Raz.)

What's a "Good Job"? MAP and YBR Meetings Enable You to Measure Employee Performance in a Meaningful Way

If you really want to drive wholesale adoption of CODE throughout your organization, here's an idea: during personal performance reviews, include measures specific to CODE, particularly farming and hunting efforts. You can easily look at six months' of weekly Whites assigned to a particular employee and directly measure their effectiveness in increasing the company's bottom line. When you give employees such clear and specific expectations, you take the mystery out of what "doing a good job" looks like for them and for the company.

Instead of telling employee something vague like, "You do a great job talking to customers," say something meaningful like, "Over the past six months, you approached 75 relational targets (Whites), which eventually resulted in $2.5 million in closed sales (Greens), with 12 more opportunities still in the pipeline (Yellows, Blues and Reds). You directly increased our profits by $225,000." Which feedback option would make you feel more proud of your work? Motivate your employees by showing hard numbers to reflect how vital and effective the company views their efforts.

With CODE, employees can take ownership of the company's success. They know that the same stick that measures corporate success measures their own. When you need to provide constructive feedback, it will not surprise the employee. After all, your team has been assigning specific tasks all along the way. Because CODE naturally keeps such clear documentation on employee's workflow as it relates to company sales, you can more easily pinpoint the root of problems (attitudes, skills or behavior modifications) and create from them constructive, measurable solutions.

- Hold MAP Whites meetings to strategize and review your progress in building relationships with new and potential customers.

- Hold YBR meetings to discuss next steps for opportunities currently in your pipeline.

- Make sure company leadership attends these meetings and participates.

- Use strategic partnerships with vendors and other companies, as well as your employees' personal connections, to find creative relational routes to the people on your MAP you want to know.

- During the transition to CODE, focus first on farming your top customers. Then transition your team to hunting for new ones.

- Train your team in conversational skills for networking events and for sales interactions with customers. At events, partner savvy, extroverted, experienced salespeople with more timid technical experts to help boost their interpersonal confidence.

- Design your employee performance reviews around CODE metrics, particularly farming and hunting efforts. This ties your employees' bar for personal success directly to the company's bar for corporate success: building positive customer relationships and sustaining loyalty.

Chapter Ten: CODE and Technology

Here is a true story shared with me by a CEO, starting with the punch line: "I spent a million dollars on a CRM and all I got was this lousy t-shirt." Yes, one company actually did that. A national bank looked at existing CRM options; none matched their needs. They hired the best qualified person to create an entirely customized CRM. Several years, a million dollars, and a disastrous failed implementation later, they abandoned the project. Next, they took many of their senior managers to a landfill, where they symbolically "buried" the CRM and handed out t-shirts to mark the occasion. Lesson learned—painfully!

Have you ever had such a frustrating experience with technology? While the rate of success is improving, CRM implementation still fails too often. There's a huge gap between the way employees do their jobs and the structure of many technologies. There are technical problems, business process problems, cultural mismatch problems and the hairy monster itself: deployment and implementation. Given such a bleak picture, it amazes me how effectively tech companies sweet-talk executives into purchasing products that fail the majority of the time. Who in their right mind would buy such a thing?

For the sake of argument, let's say that a CRM technology you've chosen to manage client relationships is the Holy Grail of computing. It came from heaven in a ray of golden gigabit sunshine, installed itself to your systems and gave you the magical key to solving every conceivable documentable or computable problem in your company.

Guess what? Your employees might still hate it. You might still end up burying it in a landfill.

Every IT department struggles with this problem. It's called "user adoption" and, more broadly, "compliance." No matter what technology you identify and plead for your workforce to adopt, chances are a significant number of them will resist it. So what's the problem? Not technology, but psychology.

What's the real problem with user adoption?

Sense of control

People hate change when it's not their idea. Sure, they will line up for hours to get the latest iPhone or tablet. They *love* the new technology. Yet, those same diehards drag their feet when there's a rollout of a new phone system at the office. People will quickly install the latest apps to their phones, but complain whenever the software at work gets a facelift. The difference? People feel control over their personal technology. To change or upgrade reflects an expression of one's being.

Work technology, on the other hand, is something employees have little control over. Higher-ups impose it in order to make the employees' actions more uniform, not more unique. People choose personal technology to increase self-expression; employers choose work technology to funnel that expression into compliance. The very psychology that makes people *like* buying an iPhone makes them resist being given the same technology at work.

Risk

When people sense risk, they feel anxiety. When I explore a new gadget on my own time, it carries little risk. When I wrestle with new software at work, my ability to complete the tasks that make me feel secure in my job feels squeezed. Sure, in the long run, the new software might be worth it, but why take the risk? What's in it for me?

No benefit to the user being forced to adopt the technology

It doesn't benefit an employee to be forced to add "data entry" to their duties, all so someone several levels above them can run data analytics and create pretty charts about company performance. The manager creating those colorful reports gets the benefit of the low price of several hundred employee hours a week—a cost their data-driven technology actively hides from them.

Consequently, companies like Apple intentionally design personal technology to benefit the user. CRM companies design corporate technology to benefit the executive who will buy the product, but not the employees he or she will have to cajole into adopting the technology. Eventually, the adoption fails, baffling and eventually angering the executives who poured so much time and money into trying to implement the new system.

Sense of waste or time pressure

Company leaders often don't realize the employee-hour cost of using the technology. However, employees do. Employees must now do their "real" job *and* spend X amount of hours messing with the technology. With a twinge of anger (or more), they feel taken advantage of as they immediately realize, "My workload is increasing." In their minds, the employment contract has suddenly changed without their consent—and not in their favor. Trust is broken, not built.

Group-think and team loyalties

Instead of functioning as one team, many companies work as a collection of several teams or interpersonal groups. Psychologically, people naturally form relationships and alliances (by department, organizational layer, location, relational cohort, etc.). People feel a greater sense of worth, security and purpose when they are part of a group. These groups aren't always immediately discernable from an organizational chart.

In a healthy company, various groups relate to each other in mutually beneficial ways. They maintain and nurture open lines of communication, according to the depth of relationship and trust each group has earned. In an unhealthy company, groups can (and do) experience communication breakdowns that lead to tit-for-tat, hidden wars with each other. Teamwork can turn into tribal warfare.

Two natural groups in any company are the managers and the employees. If you are introducing the technology, you typically originate from a different group than the adopters. Guess what? The first hurdle you'll face is that you have to sell the technology's value to those expected to use it. If instead you try to impose it by cultural or psychological force, you might meet resistance, no matter how strong the overall health of your company culture.

The first sale you will ever make with CODE is selling it to your employees.

How do you introduce something like CODE in a way that works *with* rather than *against* the psychological realties I describe above? Those realities apply as much to introducing CODE as they do to introducing new software like 1BLACKBOOK™.

The good news is that CODE is primarily *a shift in cultural mindset*, a roadmap to creating the kind of relationship culture you've always wanted. Culture must match business practices, which must match technology. That's where you'll find the sweet spot of efficient synergy.

Here are a few tips for introducing CODE, 1BLACKBOOK™ or any other new technology or business process:

- **Don't force people to accept it.** Start with a team or group of early adopters. You'll need at least some of these people to be from the target interpersonal "group"—

employees, not managers. They'll help you work out the bugs before you roll it out to the larger group. Early adopters choose to opt-in (sense of control), they have a say in how the new process gets deployed (again, sense of control), and they'll be natural "inside sellers" who show their peers how much easier the new deal makes their workload. Their example will help others see the benefits before they have to invest their time to learn and use it.

- **Make sure the benefit to the employee is clear and obvious.** If there is no clear benefit to the employee, chances are that your implementation will be rough or fail altogether. We've emphasized the clear benefits to the employee if they use CODE. We've even included a letter to employees at the back of the book, directly spelling out how CODE can benefit them. Communicate these benefits to your employees from the beginning.

- **Don't lie about the benefit to the employee.** Be honest with employees about how it will benefit them and what it will cost, what risks they will have to take, and what they stand to gain. Give the employees clear, measurable expectations and emphasize the clear ROI for them if they adopt CODE. Honesty is the foundation for building trust. Trust precedes action.

- **Implement CODE in a way that serves the worker more than the company.** If you want your employees to adopt CODE, emphasize the ways CODE give employees marketable skills and tools. Be more serious about this than you are about how CODE will increase your corporate sales. Approach the entire deployment from the perspective of solving the employees' problem of economic security, and then talk about using CODE to solve the company's revenue problem. If you get people using CODE to solve their problems, they'll be far more willing to use it to solve yours. With 1BLACKBOOK™, every employee who signs up is immediately given their own set of CODE tools. They can start using CODE in their own lives and seeing how it impacts their bottom line, as well as the company's.

CODE is a business process built on organizational psychology. How do you integrate it with technology?

Basically, there are three options:

- Go solo. Keep your technology, tweaking it to build your own MAP and YBR.

- Go hybrid. Keep your technology, but add some bolt-on apps from us to enhance your ability to create and manage your MAP and YBR (for example, our app for Salesforce).

- Make the switch. Use our technology which is a standalone solution: 1BLACKBOOK™.

Before you think about what technology to use, halt! Understand this: **No technology, not even custom Holy Grail technology, can change your sales culture.**

Technology can only enhance the culture *already* pulsing through your organization. If you have disorganization, interpersonal dysfunction and a poor reputation with clients, guess what? You need *more* than synchronized calendaring. You need a fundamental, deeply rooted culture change. That's what CODE provides. To energize that culture change through CODE, use technology that works *with* rather than *against* your target culture and business processes.

A fellow entrepreneur, Brian Hattaway, founded ProCore Resource Group, a consulting company that specializes in implementing IT solutions for businesses. Before founding ProCore, he worked with Anderson Consulting (now Accenture) as a technology architect. ProCore is a partner of Salesforce.com, the world's largest provider of software-as-service. Here is how Brian weighed in on CRMs:

"I spent a good portion of my time trying to understand why a lot of clients' system implementations failed. I found they often failed because people weren't paying attention to their business processes. You can have the best implementation team in the world, but if you can't tell me what it is you want us to build for you, I can't build it.

"We do consulting for a lot of companies and many of them just don't have a process. They may have a bunch of cowboys or Lone Ranger-type of salespeople who have had success, but they haven't consolidated all the different views and methodologies. Until they reach that point, there's no common definition of success, they can't build a predictable sales funnel and management reporting makes no sense."

Your technology and process have to reinforce each other. Use CODE to change your *culture*. As you implement it, use technology (yours or ours) to reinforce the culture you are building. Maybe your company actually has a working technology that you love. You just want to improve your sales process. At a minimum, you need these features:

The MAP

Your technological solution needs to include who you know, who you want to know, organizations to which they are connected, and how your employees' relationships follow a web of connections to these targets. You need a way to rate the targets' relationships on a 1-5 scale, based on how they currently interact with your company. You need to add notes about the targets and to easily assign to employees' White Lists the people they need to contact. You also need to be able to analyze this data to see how much progress you are making. How many 1's have turned into 2's in the past six months? Who has been most successful at contacting their White Lists? Measure these things so you can drive accountability with the MAP and see your overall progress over time in building client relationships.

The YBR

You need to be able to organize your sales pipeline by opportunity and key contact, and to color-code opportunities and search/sort by color, revenue, employee assigned to take the next step, etc. To assure accountability and measure progress, you need to analyze your success rate at every level of the YBR to discern patterns, good and bad. You need to be able to analyze data specific to employees and reporting teams to learn what works for the broader organization.

A Way to Keep Score

The beauty of CODE is that it provides everyone in the organization a uniform vocabulary by which to define success. In 1BLACKBOOK™, there is a scorecard that offers activity summaries at a glance for both personal and professional users. The seamless interaction of the MAP and the YBR allows for simple reporting metrics to evaluate performance by person, department or company. Each week, the administrator or sales manager needs to evaluate cumulative data, including total numbers of new Yellows, Blues and Reds produced weekly by person or department, percentage of opportunity in the pipeline at margin goals, weekly new 4's or 5's in relational rankings, total completed White calls made, and percentage to quota or commissions per person.

Interaction between the MAP and the YBR

The MAP is about people, and the YBR is about projects and leads in the pipeline. With CODE, the two come together in a measurable, accountable way. Your technology must integrate the data from sales in order to update the ROI associated with each relationship. That is how you will see the clearest picture of what is happening in your client relationships. You'll know where the fruit comes from, not just by account or purchase, but by level of relational influence—what I call "social currency." For tiny companies (under 20 employees), this can be done through Excel, if you have someone savvy enough to build the spreadsheets to spec, and your users are willing to work with the MAP and the YBR in that layout. However, we don't recommend that solution.

It's not very scalable, and it's hard to build tools into the company's spreadsheets that are entirely for the employees' benefit.

Instead, we advise that you put your energy into building your company's relationships and sales culture. If you are building a CODE culture, we already provide you with a technology that will match both your culture and sales process. That technology is 1BLACKBOOK™.

1BLACKBOOK™

People do business with people they like. And, people do business with people they trust.

Whether it serves as your full-fledged relational technology or as a bolt-on app to your CRM, 1BLACKBOOK™ enables you to build relationships, sales and trust with clients and employees alike.

Don't underestimate the value of having a technology system that mirrors the psychology of why you do what you do and how you do it. We created CODE by studying the psychology of sales. We watched how people behaved relationally and then expressed that in the technology of 1BLACKBOOK™, rather than trying to pigeonhole people's behaviors into algorithmic processes as is often the case with CRMs.

People + Projects = Profit

Technology and big data have created a world where everything is measurable, including relationships and relational ROI. To realize the profit you seek from managing your relationships with clients, synergize your corporate culture, business process and technology around measuring relational ROI first and profits second. Study the clear cause-and-effect links between the two. That's what CODE and 1BLACKBOOK™ do: birth sales by creating the real "customer service" culture your PR hounds have been preaching for decades.

We created 1BLACKBOOK™ to help companies adopt CODE and build relationships that turn into sales. But we also created

1BLACKBOOK™ to help you, the employee, create opportunities for yourself.

If you've ever wondered what the meaning of life is, try this: relationships. The golden rule is to "love your neighbor as yourself." We live for relationships, and so should our companies. CODE and 1BLACKBOOK™ help companies build profits by building healthy relationships with customers. They can help you do the same for yourself.

Build the foundation of every project you undertake in life on the bedrock of the relationships you've secured with trust. When you look back, those relationships will be your legacy.

- User adoption is the number one reason CRMs implementations fail at least half the time.

- People resist technology change at work. Key reasons include feelings of lack of control, forced compliance, risk to their current workflow, an increased workload with no benefit to the user, wasted time and loyalty to their own group's way of thinking, not management's.

- The first sale you will ever make with CODE is selling it to your employees.

- Don't force people to accept it. Instead, start with a team of early adapters. Make the benefit to the employee is clear and obvious (and don't lie about it). Implement CODE in a way that serves the worker more than the company.

- Choose a technology that reinforces CODE: use your own, go hybrid by adding a few apps or make the switch to our solution: 1BLACKBOOK.

- No technology, not even custom Holy Grail technology, can change your sales culture; it can only enhance the culture already pulsing through your organization.

- For your technology to enhance CODE, it must include a MAP, a YBR that interacts with the MAP and a way to keep score at the granular level.

- Relationships give employees purpose in their work. And people + projects = profit.

Afterword

I love entrepreneurs and the companies they create. In fact, I'm obsessed with them. It's for this reason I've invested the focus of my life's work in trying to understand *exactly* how entrepreneurial rainmakers operate. Are entrepreneurs as "special" as the world pretends? Or are they ordinary people like you and me who give themselves permission to try—and *do*? I believe they are the latter. Personally, I am a classic example of an accidental entrepreneur. *I didn't plan on this.* I was laid off in my early twenties, and I decided I would not let it happen again. That is why I've been working for myself ever since.

What's your story? What's your motivation?

If you've made it to this point in the book, we most likely connect in the area of entrepreneurial passion. That's why I want to point out a very disturbing trend: *According to the Babson Institute, entrepreneurism in the United States is at a three-year low.*

This deeply concerns me, as I believe entrepreneurism is the backbone of the American economy. It's the job-creation engine we depend on, and our birthright as a country. In an increasingly divided world, I believe we can collectively agree on the value entrepreneurism provides us as a people. It unites us. Inspires us. Empowers us. It reignites hope and creates job opportunity where none existed. Right now, it's estimated that 23 million people in job transition need this hope. What are we doing as business owners and corporate leaders?

Part of my personal response to this question is my life's work, as contained in this book. I didn't write *Driving Demand* because I needed a new hobby. I wrote it because I believe that people must acquire and develop entrepreneurial skills for the betterment of the world and economy. This is my life's purpose and mission. It's why I'm here.

Today, the majority of people in the U.S. think America is on the wrong track. What contributes to that notion? I believe one factor is the declining state of entrepreneurism. This is why I conclude this book by inviting you to join me in a movement designed to reignite entrepreneurial thinking and empowerment.

At 1BLACKBOOK™, our mission is to add measurable economic value to everyone we touch. For every business license we sell, we plan to accomplish to offer a free license, training, prayer and community support to a long-term unemployed person who needs to learn what it takes to become an Economy of One, through a network of non-profit partners.

In addition to adding measurable value to our corporate partners, we are committed to creating a battle line with which business leaders can engage in the war to retain skilled labor and reinsert people into the job market. Today, it is estimated that 3.7 million good jobs exist, yet the wrong people are applying for these "right and real jobs." While a significant skills gap does exist, it is widely recognized that up to 80% of real jobs aren't posted. We believe by teaching people to better farm and hunt in their own networks of friends, we can uncover a ground swell of new employment opportunities and re-engagement.

In 2012, the U.S. government claimed to have created 250,000 jobs.[18] **Imagine if we can fill just 10% of the 3.7 million jobs that are currently open with a new and innovative solution.**

---

[18] Cauchon, Dennis. "Federal Employment Drops after Years of Explosive Growth." *USA Today*. 6 June 2012. Web. 26 Oct. 2014.

If we could, we would be able to top government productivity at "creating jobs." We could collectively say, "We built this."

This is my dream and aim of my company, 1BLACKBOOK™. **Will you join me in the fight?** America and the world need to re-ignite their entrepreneurial engines by teaching people that money is anything we can use to solve a problem for someone else. With this definition of wealth, we are infinitely rich and can do so much more to imagine new ways to engage.

We can do more as business leaders. We can do more as a nation. **We are an Economy of One.**

God bless you,

Elizabeth Allen

Founder & CEO, 1BLACKBOOK™
Kansas City

Tips & Tools

Implementation Tips

TIP #1: What might role assignments look like, depending on the size of the organization?

- **Small organizations**, including one-person-bands or "solo-preneurs," might call for an "all hands on deck" approach, where everyone in the company acts as Prospectors for farming and hunting, and also as Technical Experts and/or Closers.

- **Mid-sized organizations** divide their roles and responsibilities more distinctly. Depending on the expertise of the sales or business development people (their level of technical skills or authority to close), they might be assigned purely the role of Prospector, leaving the technical qualification and closing to others.

- **Enterprise-sized organizations**, defined by individuals, departments or divisions, will assign roles depending upon the goals of the organization. The principles of CODE will remain constant, but the process and execution will be specific to certain goals or product lines. Companies adapt CODE to fit their needs.

TIP #2: What questions should management consider to start assigning roles?

- Who is currently acting as Prospectors, Technical Experts, or Closers?

- Who would be "in the know" about new business?

- Who is in frequent contact (of any kind) with core customers?

- Who is appropriate to qualify the scope of projects or service opportunities?

- Who has the authority (and ability) to negotiate and close?

- Who is identified as the face of the organization?

- Who is working on strategic issues?

TIP #3: What are some suggestions for how employees might approach established and potential customers to farm and hunt for their business?

- Call customers and sincerely thank them for their business. Check their overall satisfaction with the services or project you performed. Inquire about plans for moving forward. Ask if they know of other companies that might require your services (referrals). Let them know when you will be back in touch.

- Drive greater loyalty by addressing any perceived advantages associated with the known competition. Intentionally push toward becoming a client's single source by asking questions like, "What can we do to provide more value to you?"

- Nurture the relationship toward identifying specific opportunities.

- Send a referral to the client and reciprocate with them in terms of professional favors. Give at least twice to people before you ask for a favor in return. Look for ways to add value, or send them a nice introduction to let them know you appreciate them. Keep in mind that "social currency" is any informational asset that transfers measurable economic value to one or both parties. Get creative with how you use what you know to strategically help people and nurture relationships.

- Get to know the company or contact, establish a relationship, and eventually size up possible opportunities. Confirm that the contact is indeed qualified to be a prospect.

TIP #4: What to Expect During the Change Process (Week-by-Week Summary)

Weeks 1-6: Leadership creates a basic understanding of the CODE process among employees and begins shifting everyone to a new mindset as the organization adapts CODE to the system of operation. If a new technology such as 1BLACKBOOK™ is used, then leadership provides employees with access to our eLearning tools for CODE and their own subscriptions to 1BLACKBOOK™. If existing technology is adapted, then management uses CODE to help teach employees about the CODE process, roles and responsibilities.

Weeks 7-12: Enterprise-wide adoption of the new vocabulary and process. Employees have started using CODE in some measurable sales efforts. Leadership and employees are both using the MAP and the YBR. Prospectors are working from weekly White Lists, either produced manually or automatically by the technology.

Weeks 13-18: Development of comfort and proficiency. MAP and YBR reporting comes more naturally to employees who are relying increasingly on it to direct their relational workflow.

Weeks 19-24: Push for sustained growth. Managers and teams work to maintain or improve performance levels as individual team members understand and utilize CODE in all sales efforts.

TIP #5: A Ten Point Checklist for Reviewing the Health of YBR Progress Meetings

1. Is everyone attending who should be there?

Specifically, are the company leaders present? While it's important that every team member attend, when leaders are absent, they risk undermining their ability to drive accountability to the process for all concerned. Model what you expect your employees to do.

2. Quiet defiance vs. buy-in: Can leadership tell the difference? Is upper-level management willing to address the issue if necessary?

Attitude can affect everything and everyone. It is up to leadership to set the tone and address any elephants in the room. When leaders tolerate quietly defiant behavior, the meeting can prove counterproductive for those willing to engage in the process. "One fly in the soup can spoil the meal," the old saying goes. Evidence of "quiet defiance" includes anyone who refuses to post updates or notes, who plays with their phone or email, who contributes little or nothing during the progress meetings or who attends only when he or she "feels" like it.

3. Are people using the meetings to teach others?

The MAP White meetings and YBR meetings offer opportunities for senior level executives to share "in the trenches" experiences important for cross-training junior members of the team. For instance, you might cover the reason a particular prospect needs to be handled a certain way, or why it's important to write a proposal in a specific manner. Such discussions provide junior members with key insight into time-tested strategies.

Here's an example: a company had invested 500 hours of work (equivalent to $20K) on a fairly large-scale job, only to discover they held no apparent leverage with the general contractor. One senior level executive felt the situation came down to price. He commented that no matter how much value they might add, or how many hours they might invest, it would make no difference, because they were "only" a sub-contractor.

However, another senior level executive confronted this "commodity mindset" by pointing out that a sister division had just landed a $28 million job without submitting the lowest bid. How? Because that division enjoyed an established relationship with the general contractor!

Cultural perceptions and attitudes can impact outcomes.

4. Are callback dates updated?

If leadership does not model the behavior of updating callback dates, everyone else will eventually take a hall pass, too. Again, model what you expect others to do.

5. Are team members proposing next steps—and why they plan to take them?

Most organizations will need to clarify what to enter onto the YBR in the early stages of implementing CODE. For example, a fast-moving service department may field numerous core customer service requests for tiny dollar amounts. It is not a good use of the YBR to document every piddling detail. Management must decide what baseline dollar amount is worth tracking, so that the majority will gain maximum benefit from using the YBR as a tool.

Meeting leaders should also listen for how team members are using the Eight Qualifying Questions to qualify opportunities. Does anyone need further coaching? The YBR and MAP meetings offer endless opportunities to teach. Furthermore, the meetings reveal any training your team members truly need in order to increase your company's bottom line.

6. Are the meetings focusing on SALES issues? Or are the Technical Experts veering off-topic into detailed discussions better addressed in operational or project management meetings?

Technical Experts tend to focus on their areas of expertise, rather than sales. If this happens, redirect them! Operational firefighting can derail the primary purpose of the meeting.

7. Who needs to attend every meeting?

A quick story: I worked with an electrical company whose project managers were stationed on work sites. Now and then, the managers picked up news from suppliers and vendors about possible upcoming projects. Typically, their project managers did not participate in sales qualification or closing processes, and did not attend progress meetings. However, for instances such as this, they could contribute to a discussion of new Yellows by showing up for part of a meeting or by passing on the information to members of the sales team.

8. What is the total pipeline value?

Determine if the overall pipeline value is increasing or decreasing, and why. Periodically, call the team's attention to either trend, and ask for feedback. The quality of activity and depth in the pipeline can make a big difference in setting strategy. Discussing this helps people engage with a "Big Picture" perspective. Looking at larger sales trends—a "management" concern—with employees can reinforce the level of ownership they take in the company's success. Everyone should be taking responsibility for the quality and quantity of the YBR.

9. What is the ratio of new vs. existing customers in the pipeline?

There should be a healthy mix of both, not just repeat core customers. Do you have a strategic plan to diversify into new markets? Look at how your pipeline confirms measurable progress toward that goal.

10. How is the team really doing? What have you learned about their performance? What skills or behaviors do they need to develop further? Are team members self-evaluating their scorecards and determining what the numbers and colors in the pipeline are telling them?

If new business development hires aren't making progress, my advice is for management to slow down and ask, "Why? Do they have the support they need? Has a clear goal been set, such as gaining three new Yellows, two new Blues and one new Red per week? Are their goals in sync with the expectations of leadership? Are they realistic?"

If you base your employee performance reviews on data from the MAP and the YBR, then keep this in mind as you look at the health of your meetings. Are the meetings enabling employees to meet their individual goals week to week?

Frequently Asked Questions

Are the eLearning tools and the related CRM technology for CODE available right now?

Yes. Please visit www.1BLACKBOOK.com.

Who should participate in training?

CODE is a comprehensive solution appropriate for sales and business development teams, as well as entire divisions or organizations. CODE training addresses how every person employed in an organization can support the sales process, no matter their "official title." Ideally, every employee should participate in a portion of the eLearning tools on the fundamental concepts behind CODE. In particular, everyone should go through the CODE overview and the segment about changing the cultural mindset to an "all hands on deck" approach.

When CODE is implemented across marketing and sales divisions, all marketing and sales team members should fully participate in the e-learning.

Finally, every leader responsible for driving accountability to organizational goals of any kind—sales or individual—should also be aware of details associated with the program at a high level.

Is it realistic to expect everyone to support sales?

Yes, but ultimately employees opt-in at a level or stage that is right for them. At a minimum, employees need to understand that caring for (i.e., farming) core customers is critical to the company's health and future. They can make such efforts in a variety of practical ways. To do that, employees need a clear understanding of the organization's unique Human Brand and how to communicate those qualities during every contact with customers.

What are the signs of "disconnect" when implementing the program?

Primary indicators include: lack of participation at progress meetings by management or team members; lack of meaningful dialogue or cross-learning (going off-topic or losing focus of a meeting's primary purpose); resistance to updating the YBR or the MAP; or simply a lack of measurable results. We've addressed each of these points throughout the book so you can avoid such pitfalls.

What happens if those assigned to "prospecting" aren't performing?

Performance expectations must be clearly communicated to everyone participating in the program, whether engaged in farming, hunting or both. Team leaders need to confirm each person's understanding of his or her role(s) and responsibilities. Weekly or bi-monthly progress meetings will help drive accountability to clearly defined and established goals. For example, a leader might assign a team member a written weekly goal such as, "You will be responsible for contacting three Whites and following up with two Yellows for your team."

If you have a team member who freezes up when contacting a White because they don't understand how to talk to the potential client, consider some creative training exercises. For example, you might have a savvier team member write up a sample dialogue report detailing a White conversation they had, *verbatim*. That team member can even choose one of their more difficult conversations, so you can obtain more learning fodder than you would from an "ideal" example. Direct the group to strategize about how they might have responded in such a conversation. Or, try role-playing common responses that team members get from Whites, so they can try out new approaches to dialogue in the safety of practicing with their own team. Sure, it doesn't sound academic, but people learn by doing.

How do I deal with resistance to CODE?

Keep in mind that the learning curve in adopting CODE is approximately six months. Anticipate some degree of organizational pushback in the first ten weeks, even out to 18 weeks. It may surface in a number of ways. Common indicators include:

- Influential employees who lack motivation or voice skepticism around buying into the program, behaviors that indicate quiet defiance or a general lack of focus during progress meetings.

- Leaders or sales people are seen rushing to enter data minutes before weekly meetings—something you should address head-on if you see it happen.

Address resistance the same way you would address employee resistance to any other company policy: carrot-and-stick, with respect, clear expectations and defined rewards and benefits to the employee if they come around.

What are the responsibilities of senior leaders and officers in changing our culture to embrace CODE?

Some people are naturally going to avoid change. They will default to "the norm," no matter what. Until S- or even C-level leaders demand accountability, it will be difficult, perhaps impossible, for cultural buy-in to take hold.

Top management must display a sincere, consistent and clear commitment to the core elements of the program by Communicating, Organizing, Documenting and Evaluating their company's transition to using CODE.

When leaders use CODE to fill the YBR pipeline, they encourage others to succeed with it as well. Once that happens, universal adoption is pretty rapid, as people realize, "I guess this isn't going away. I'd better adapt and yes, it's in my best long-term interest to do this." Employees mimic what leaders model.

What are the basic Farming functions?

Farming connects you with core customers or strategic partners to better serve their needs and the needs of the organization. Some farming functions and strategies include: thanking the customer for contracts and purchases; making sure the customer is satisfied; collecting industry information; working toward upcoming opportunities; and requesting referrals. If Prospectors (Farmers) are not engaging properly with customers, most likely it is because they do not understand what it means to farm. Farming does not mean "cold calling" people they don't know.

What are the basic Hunting functions?

Generally, those asked to hunt within the first few weeks of the CODE program are senior level managers, top organizational leaders, or those already associated with sales and business development. Performance issues often surface rapidly when YBR postings expose individual sales effectiveness (or ineffectiveness). Depending on the sales cycle of the product or service, results should be evident within approximately 30 days of the program launch. When dealing with issues associated with Hunters, be fair and clear in evaluating the problems. Coach and train for improved performance.

What is an example of coaching that improves Hunting performance?

Start by reviewing and clarifying expectations. Ask a few basic questions:

- Are they clear on measurable goals and timeframes for completion?

- What three issues do they perceive as barriers to their success?

- How does the goal to improve relational rankings tie into their strategy to manage the account or contact?

Coach for improvement to overcome any barriers they perceive to their success. There are many books on this subject, so I will not go into detail on how to address each issue. I do encourage scheduling weekly meetings to break down the process into measurable, incremental steps in order to help people embrace—instead of running from—their challenges.

After you've communicated helpful steps, you may still find team members deficient in certain areas. Don't be discouraged. Give them further coaching. Specific issues might include: call reluctance, poor use of time, inability to get past a gatekeeper, lack of confidence in the sales process or in the quality of your products. In any instance, management needs to provide a timeframe of support and troubleshooting to clarify the problem and help the worker. Should there be little to no change within 45 days of applying serious coaching efforts, I would suspect the person is in the wrong role.

What are some typical complaints (or excuses) you've seen during the learning and implementation process of CODE?

- "I don't have time for this. I have other responsibilities."

- "I don't really know where to start."

- "I am feeling lost."

- "I am not clear on what to pursue."

- "I just don't want to make the effort to connect with other people."

- "I am connecting but getting nowhere."

- "I'm measured by billable hours, not this."

- "I am not confident about what I'm being asked to sell."

- "I resent being asked to do this."

- "I don't feel motivated."

- "I have poor time management (and/or follow-through) skills."

As a leader, create an atmosphere where people feel comfortable voicing their thoughts openly so that you can respond directly to their complaints and fears. Chances are, someone else in the group is also "feeling lost," and needs you to review some part of the training. Model these behaviors by using CODE for yourself. Encourage your employees to step outside their comfort zone by stepping outside of yours. Give employees a grace period as they try new skills, and also give them clear expectations and measurable goals to meet.

How long does effective hunting take?

Using the MAP, targets and associated time management goals for hunters should be very concise. Once the MAP White List is used to identify a target, it usually takes a series of interactions to establish rapport and identify a viable opportunity.

If you properly orchestrate your progress meetings, you'll be able to discuss and collaborate with each other about how to hunt more effectively. Hunters tend to focus on Yellows and Reds, depending on the health of the pipeline. Set performance measures for each of these categories.

When reviewing the YBR pipeline, make sure that the Prospecting role and associated outcomes are clear. In some instances, individuals who refuse to support the effort do not understand the parameters of what you are asking them to do.

Management needs to factor the comprehension time and clarity of communication into their overall performance evaluation, since it relates to how people understand their roles and how they take action in their areas of perceived responsibility.

When do I let someone go that I hired as a pure Prospector?

Quick answer: after all efforts to provide an opportunity for success have been exhausted. I've worked with many companies who had no plans to support personnel development. They also did not convey clear, specific expectations about performance. Define what effective farming and hunting means, in specific metrics for your organization. Show employees how to do it. Use this book as a discussion platform.

CODE is a process with a learning curve. If, after 45 to 60 days, a farming Prospector has not demonstrated adequate progress, then it may be time to relieve them of their duties. On the other hand, 60 to 90 days could also serve as an appropriate timeframe to release those who have been hunting without results. It depends on the length of your sales cycle. Give people a chance to learn to succeed, and to train in the role you are asking them to fulfill.

Why do Technical Experts benefit from understanding the roles of Prospector and Closer?

Technical Experts are sometimes asked to support other roles in their sales efforts because they are often the most knowledgeable about which solutions a company can provide to meet customer's needs.

Too frequently, Technical Experts lack either an appreciation or understanding of the sales process. Some view salespeople as non-contributors to "billable" revenue. Depending on the culture of the organization, there can be tremendous disconnect between the technical and sales teams.

CODE brings all the skills and players together. It delivers respect for all, yet fosters effective cross-training of behaviors.

Your sales people can benefit in hard skills from spending time with Technical Experts, and your Technical Experts can pick up some of the soft skills for which good salesmen are known.

Does every opportunity need be recorded on the YBR?

Management has to determine a baseline dollar amount worth tracking, so that the majority benefit from using the tool. That might mean some smaller opportunities will not be recorded or tracked. Your employees do not like feeling trapped in data entry unless there is a clear payoff to their workload. Set the minimum documentation guidelines according to what the employees need in order to coordinate their sales efforts as a team—not according to a micro-managerial itch to track every conceivable detail.

We hit a plateau in performance. In some ways, we have even dropped off. What could be the problem?

If this occurs within six weeks of launching the program, then it could amount to one of two things: some don't fully understand the program; or you're dealing with organizational pushback. When you introduce something new, it takes consistency and up to six months of implementation for people to fully accept the associated cultural change.

Where can I find downloadable MAP and YBR templates?

1BLACKBOOK.com.

A Sample YBR Progress Meeting Agenda

Week 1—Executive Progress Meeting

MAP progress confirmation, YBR progress confirmation and creation of short-term plans to launch the CODE program

Meeting Agenda

- **Temperature Check**—In general, how do people feel about CODE? What are the observed changes to date? (10 min)

- **Overall Progress Reports / Each Reporting Person**—Totals in prospecting efforts, number tallies per person, clients to update (20 min)

- **YBR Reports**—Highlights of progress, executive team to choose individuals and cases to focus on, coaching comments and questions (10-15 min)

- **Troubleshooting**—Key presentations for the week of (insert date), review the point-in-process of critical Blues or Reds (10 min)

- **Identify Candidates for Coaching in upcoming week**—Prioritize sales team members we will target coaching sessions with during the next week (5 min)

- **Address any unresolved marketing issues** (5 min)

- **Review** documentation concerns, progress against short term plans and internal communication efforts

Reference for recording minutes of the meeting:

* = New Salesperson Comments
# = Calendar Note
+ = Positive Observation
- = Negative Observation
cc = Coach Comment

Start Time:

End time:

End of Meeting Temperature Check:

Dear Employees,
Here's What's in It for You...

It's not just in your head. There really are "fewer" jobs out there. Technology will soon automate out of existence up to 47% of jobs.[19] Almost half of all workers will end up floating from contract to contract as free agents (not full-time employees) by 2019.

The Russians have a proverb: "There's nothing more permanent than a 'temporary solution.'" Companies are hiring fewer and fewer full-time employees. They are using a series of temporary solutions—contract workers—and are only getting more permanently comfortable with operating that way.

Are you prepared for this shifting employment landscape? What does this mean for you and your family?

I encourage you not to let fear grip or overwhelm you. Not every industry is changing, but many are touched by advancing technologies. What's your plan?

Please let me help you change the way you may weigh the issues. Sure, the security of the old, full-time, "lifer" system is fading

---

[19] Frey, Carl, and Michael Osborne. "The Future of Employment: How Susceptible Are Jobs to Computerisation?" University of Oxford. 17 Sept. 2013. Web. 12 Oct. 2014.

away. But, you're about to have a lot more power over your career than you ever did before. You are about to gain those "mysterious" skills that those alien, outlier, wildly successful entrepreneurs all seem to possess. You're going to enjoy increased confidence and know what is required (step by step) to sell yourself and identify the new opportunities you need. You're going to have a network that fills your plate with a pipeline of op-options. More people will be able to decide when they work, with whom they work and for how much.

Generally, that's the upside the global economic shift. As the free agent culture takes over the world, *even if you are full-time permanent*, the change in the climate will make you feel like a "mini company" working with your employer. That's actually what an independent contractor already is. And it does have its perks.

Make up your mind—right now—to consider the merits of the sales process your employer is about to implement. Here's what is in it for you:

- An exit strategy if by chance you ever need one

- Clear expectations and a greater ability to see the real impact of your labor

- More power to defend your value in performance reviews and negotiate for what you need to be successful in your career

CODE will teach you to manage relationships and turn them into opportunities. That skill will open up tremendous possibilities for you and your employer, now and in the future.

Exit Strategy

Everyone likes to feel like they have options. This program will teach you to build a network, and to sell and fill a pipeline with opportunities. You can use these same skills to build your personal network, to "sell" your abilities and win a new job or contract and to keep your own pipeline full with opportunities for work. Why not structure your career like a business? Benefit from the same principles that make "business owner" one of the most profitable—and enviable—job titles in the country.

There may be someone else in your life who needs an exit strategy, such as the recent college graduate now living in your basement. You've been telling him to get a job for six months after warning him not to major in English. Your wife has had it up to her eyeballs with the video games streaming from what your son affectionately calls his "man cave."

Let's teach you *the skills you need to help get that kid an internship* (read: job creator), a contract or even an entry-level position. Pass these skills on to your kid so he can finally launch into the independence you dreamed he'd have since that first 2 a.m. diaper change a quarter of a century ago.

Clear Expectations and a Greater Ability to See the Real Impact of Your Labor

With CODE, your employer will lay out very clear expectations. For example, "Call Mike, Juan and Sarah." You'll have a voice in picking who your Mikes, Juans and Sarahs are, according to your level of participation. Your whole team will be doing a little bit of this. You'll choose the roles you are comfortable with, and your company will track the results of your overall opportunity.

The MAP and the YBR will make your work life much more predictable and less stressful. No one will expect you to magically produce sales out of thin air. You won't have to worry about the talk around the water cooler of how well—*or not*—the company seems to be doing or about whether that might mean layoffs for your team like it did for your buddy Joe at that other company down the street. You'll have a few calls to make and then you'll be able to sit back and ignore the fear-mongering pinging at you from news outlets ("Unemployment up 1%").

You'll be able to focus on getting your technical work done and spending the majority of your time doing what you've always done best. You'll know exactly how much value, in real dollars, your work produces for the company. Instead of pushing paper, you'll be able to directly see and measure what your efforts produce. Work will feel more meaningful because the company is about to highlight your successes to a degree that even the healthiest ego might feel bashful about.

Nothing fosters worker appreciation more than rainmaking. It's practically impossible to fire rainmakers. (Out of rain comes lighting.) You'll be able to tie your immediate labor to direct increases in the company's profits (and maybe even your stock portfolio, if you own company stock). What do you think will that do for your résumé and hireability as you move forward in your career?

More Power to Defend Your Value in Performance Reviews and Negotiate for What You Need to Be Successful in Your Career

During your employee performance review, you won't have to deal with vague statements. You'll be able to walk in, ready to say things like, "I contacted 35 people over the past quarter. The rest of the team followed up and did their part, and ultimately, the company got $1.5 million in revenue out of it. That's what my team and I produced for the company, just from the few clients I contacted each week. Five projects that would never have existed for us got done because of my initiative."

Your managers will be working with you along the way so that, even between performance reviews, your value will be clearly seen by those above you on a weekly basis. The confidence of knowing you will be acknowledged for doing a very specific set of defined tasks will take a lot of mystery and politicking out of measuring your value. It will restore your sense of job security. You might be surprised at just how much such clear expectations will reduce your anxiety in this economic climate.

CODE's main tools—the MAP, and the Yellow-Blue-Red (YBR) pipeline of opportunities—create natural, reasonable expectations for each team member. You won't have to worry about whom your manager happens to play favorites with, because you'll back up your value to the company's bottom line with hard numbers. They mean a lot more to the company than the number of hours you worked. Wouldn't you rather be measured by the quality of what you produce, instead of the number of Friday nights you spent at the office?

With a clear and obvious way to defend your value, you can steer your mental energies away from worrying and toward furthering the success of your career. When you can back up your value with the confidence of clear data, you can negotiate more easily for the tools, training and opportunities you want to increase your skills and value to the company.

There are also some solid economics as to why mastering CODE will increase your wages, even beyond the obvious reason that it makes the company profitable. When you can easily drum up better-paying work for yourself elsewhere, your employer has to pay more to keep you from leaving and going to the competition. Intuitively, they know this. Pay is largely influenced by two factors:

- How much would it cost to hire someone else to do this job just as well?

- What would it cost us if this person left and went to the competition?

In the world of attorneys, there is a question: "When do you make someone partner?"

The answer? "When they can gut the firm of clients if they leave."

CODE will make you less expendable, and your employer knows it. Suddenly, Marjory, that secretary down the hall who was about to be automated out of existence, looks a lot more valuable. Why? Because her cousin, Jacob, works for the key decision-maker at a major core customer. Jacob went to school with at least five key decision-makers at other companies; that's just who you've identified so far. The company Christmas party is coming up in four months, and Marjory has already invited Jacob. Her manager sees this on the MAP and quietly thinks to himself, "Marjory can't run Excel to save her life, but heck if I'm replacing her anytime soon..."

Here's another example from an HR manager's meeting. "Peter's been here ten years. We could probably hire a young kid just out of school who's up on the latest engineering technology. The kid would probably even be willing to work weekends. He'd be so happy for a full-time, permanent job in this economy. We'd only have to pay him half as much.

"On the other hand, most of those kid's connections are fresh out of school. Peter's friends are decision-makers and influencers at the heights of their careers. Look at the MAP. Before CODE, we would never have known it, but one-third of our division's business last year involved at least one of Peter's contacts at some point in the bidding process. That's several million dollars in sales, of which $750,000 originated from just two contacts. Peter got the ball rolling on both of those by making the initial phone call to inquire about possible opportunities.

"From the numbers, it looks like we'd lose far more money in business to the competition than we'd save by replacing him with the young graduate. Let's highlight his success at the next staff meeting. Maybe it will motivate some of the others who are still passively engaged."

CODE Brings Power to Employees and Profit to Companies

If you're with me so far, take a look at the next section. I've put in a cheat sheet for how you can take advantage of CODE for your personal use. For years, I've worked as a sales consultant to different companies. With the structural changes that happened to the economy during that time, I've seen individuals and industries go through some sincere pain.

My husband, an electrical engineer, was laid off from a Fortune 500 company after decades of faithful service because they closed his plant to consolidate production. When that happened, we used CODE to make the transition. He lined up a pipeline of opportunities. At first, we had to build traction with a lot of networking. Then it took on a life of its own, and he became able to pick and choose his contracts—when he works, for whom he works, and for what price. He's able to set his own schedule, a freedom from which our family really benefits, since we've still got two young kids at home.

Take a look at the cheat sheet on the next page. My hope is that CODE will create the same freedom for you that it has for us. I've written another book dedicated to this process for free agents. It's called *The Economy of One*. I encourage you to pick it up at a library or on Amazon.

Cheat Sheet: CODE Snapshot for Personal Use

Define the Product

Take an inventory of all your skills. Include your education, experience, and hobbies. Include every resource you can use to define solutions that you can provide to others. You are now a small business, an economy of one, selling your skills to the world. If you've been laid off, your next opportunity might look very different from the last, so include *every* marketable skill you have.

MAP (Marketing Action Plan): Who You Know and Who You Want to Know

Make a list of everyone you know. *Everyone.* Now, make a 'dream list' of everyone you'd like to know. Who do you need to meet to create the opportunities you deserve? Wherever you can't think of specific names, create a detailed description of who you want to know and their associated companies or industries, so that you can ask others for appropriate introductions.

YBR (Yellow, Blue, Red): Your Pipeline of Possible Opportunities

Stop funneling your energy into anxiety. Instead, use it to contact people from your MAP. These are your Whites. Contact a certain number of whites every week and inquire about possible opportunities that would match any of the solutions your skills could enable you to provide. Don't be shy about asking your contacts to make an introduction to someone they know who might be in a better position to tell you about an opportunity. Keep in mind that 80% of jobs aren't posted, and that your odds of landing a job from an online application are 1 in 1,000. When submitted by someone familiar with the opportunity, the odds of your resume resulting in a hire jump to 1 in 7. Classify every opportunity according to a color-coded status:

- **Yellow** = possible. You're not sure if the prospect has a timeline or a budget to hire or purchase a solution, but based on the industry or company, you suspect an opportunity might exist.

- **Blue** = definite. The prospect has a budget and timeline for getting the kind of solution you might be able to provide. They are willing to meet with you to see if you are a good fit for each other. Slow down, ask a lot of questions, think like a Technical Expert to establish your value, and vet the opportunity.

- **Red** = moving toward a close. The prospect has met with you and wants to make a deal. Think like a Closer.

Three Roles: Prospector, Technical Expert and Closer

When you are 'farming' relationships you already have and 'hunting' for introductions you need, you are prospecting for opportunities. It's all about building relationships and meeting people. Once you have a Yellow or Blue opportunity, transition yourself into thinking like a Technical Expert. Slow down and check things out. Find out what the opportunity specifically needs, and be honest about the value you can provide. You don't just want any opportunity—you want something that's a good fit for both sides.

When the prospect is ready to make a deal, have the courage to become a Closer. Make a direct ask or otherwise come to a clear, yes-or-no agreement with defined terms. Whether you win the opportunity or not, be sure to follow-up later to maintain the relationship (Greens that transfer back to your MAP). You never know where it might lead in the future. Keep track of your progress in generating leads (Yellows, Blues and Red) and be honest about where you struggle in the process. Improve your interpersonal communication and your success rate.

Remember, you have one goal: to keep your opportunity pipeline filled and moving forward, predictably. The only way you can do that in the long-term is to focus on cultivating lasting relationships and build trust. Then you will be able to convert those relationships to win-win opportunities.

If you approach how you create income streams by adopting the mindset of nurturing relationships, those relationships will become not just a source of income, but also the legacy of your professional life. As one very famous sales book proclaims, *Go-Givers Sell More.*

If you would like more information on how to apply CODE for personal use, please see *The Economy of One: CODE for Free Agents* at Amazon.com.

22120056R00105

Made in the USA
San Bernardino, CA
21 June 2015